I0559706

EDITIONS PARTS AND SUPERTITLES

978-1-963088-04-5	Moses Facing Jordan Full Score
978-1-963088-05-2	Moses Facing Jordan Piano/Vocal, German
978-1-963088-06-9	Moses Facing Jordan Piano/Vocal, Dutch
Contact publisher	Orchestra Parts Rental
Contact publisher	English/German Supertitles for Projection
Contact publisher	English/Dutch Supertitles for Projection
Contact publisher	Supertitles in other languages

WILLIAM COPPER

MOSES
Facing Jordan

Libretto from the Books of Moses
compiled by William Copper

Oratorio in Two Acts

Piano/Vocal Score

Übertitel auf Deutsch

Orchestra
(2121-0320-Tmp-Strings)
Mixed Chorus
Tenor and Bass-baritone Soloists

HARTENSHIELD MUSIC

HARTENSHIELD GROUP, INC.
Chicago IL USA

Copyright © 2024 by William Copper
All rights reserved.

Piano reduction and music engraving by the composer.

Printed in the United States of America

Libretto Copyright © 2022 William Copper
Supertitles in German © 2024 William Copper

ISBN: 978-1-963088-05-2 Paperback
ISMN: 979-0-800337-00-0

Hartenshield Group, Inc.
12 East Scott Street #12-3
Chicago IL 60610

CONTENTS

Performance Notes		v
Orchestra		vii

Part I. At the Jordan River: You shall be gathered to your people

No. 1	Introduction	1
	Go up into this mountain	
No. 2	Scene	9
	And I besought the Lord	
No. 3	Fugue	13
	Thou shalt not go	

Part II. At the Side of the Wilderness: God called to him

No. 4	Recitative	23
	Now Moses led the flock	
No. 5	Aria	24
	And the angel of the Lord	
No. 6	Scene	29
	When the Lord saw	
No. 7	Chorale	33
	I have seen the affliction	
No. 8	Caravanserai	35
	Who am I?	
No. 9	Fugue	38
	Say this, I AM THAT I AM	
No. 10	Recitative	46
	Oh, my Lord, I am not eloquent	

Part III. The Successes of Moses: How fair are your tents

No. 11	Chorale	47
	How fair are your tents, O Jacob	
No. 12	Recitative	50
	The oracle of Balaam	
No. 13	Chorus	51
	He has not beheld misfortune	
No. 14	Recitative	62
	Then Sion came out	
No. 15	Chorus	63
	And the Lord delivered him	
No. 16	Recitative	75
	Then Og the King of Bashan came out	
No. 17	Chorale	75
	Do not fear him	

Part IV. The Laws: Surely this great nation

No. 18	Recitative	77
	Behold I have taught you	
No. 19	Canon	78
	Thou shalt have no other god	
No. 20	Recitative	87
	Keep therefore and do them	
No. 21	Chorus	88
	Surely this great nation	

Part V. The Troubles: They weep unto me, thy people

No. 22	Rondo	105
	The Lord look upon you and judge	
No. 23	Plaint	113
	Why hast thou dealt ill	
No. 24	Chorale	118
	Up! Make us gods.	
No. 25	Chorus	120
	And the men who were the heads	
No. 26	Chorus	122
	Would that we had died	

Part VI. Face to Face: I brought you on eagles's wings

No. 27	Recitative	137
	And Moses went up	
No. 28	Chorale	138
	Eagles, on eagles	
No. 29	Chorus	141
	Give ear, o ye heavens	
No. 30	Paean	150
	For ask now	

Part VII. Miriam Sang: Sing to the Lord gloriously

No. 31	Celebration	154
	Sing to the Lord	
No. 32	Scene	164
	Behold I will strike the water	
No. 33	Scene	180
	How long refuse us?	
No. 34	March	187
	Darkness	
No. 35	Recitative	192
	At midnight the Lord	
No. 36	Scene	194
	Then did Pharaoh's daughter	

PERFORMANCE NOTES

THE ECTATIC, tenor

The visionary historian telling parts of the story of the Life of Moses

MOSES, bass-baritone

At the end of his life, approaching the Jordan River, Moses remembers his own life from this moment back to his discovery in the Nile River by the daughter of Pharaoh, who drew him from the waters.

CHORUS

Soprano Alto
Tenor   Bass

This work employs just intonation in various keys. Where notes deviate from basic tuning, modified accidentals have been provided. The key signature defines the basic tuning, with all notes having a relationship to the tonic as indicated by the key.

When a changing harmony requires deviations, modified accidentals are used: sharps and flats with arrows up or down, and neutral accidentals that are small arrows up or down and specify tuning but do not alter the note spelling. In each case, the arrow indicates a change in tuning by an adjustment of approximately 22 cents, known as the 'comma of Didymus'. The purpose of all markings is to help the musicians find the pure tuning planned at every moment of music.

All accidentals, including modified and neutral markings, apply to the measure within which they are found; they are followed when appropriate by a courtesy accidental in the next measure.

In a particular key, the standard diatonic tuning for just intonation, when no special markings are encountered, is specifically: a tonic note, its pure fifth above and below (the dominant and subdominant), and the major third, seventh, and sixth (the mediant, leading tone, and submediant) tuned to each respective tonal note in pure major thirds. The supertonic changes most frequently with the unmarked version a pure fifth above the dominant and a version indicated with a neutral down arrow most often used in various subdominant harmonies.

Chromatic notes outside the indicated key signature when unmarked are always in pure fifth relations to the leading tone of the key, when sharper than the key, and in pure fifth relations to the subdominant of the key, when flatter than the key. For example in C major, an F# with no modification of the accidental is a pure fifth above B and Bb with no modification of the accidental is a pure fifth below F.

ORCHESTRA

2 Flutes
Oboe
Clarinet
Bassoon

3 Trumpets
2 Trombones

Timpani

Violin I
Violin II
Viola
Violoncello
Double bass

Moses Facing Jordan

Libretto from the Books of Moses

William Copper

PART I. At the Jordan River: You shall be gathered to your people

#1 Introduction Go Up Into this Mountain

Allegro Maestoso ($\quarternote$=108-112)

Piano
Reduction

0566

(1) Steige auf! Gehe auf diesen Berg
Go up! Go up into this mountain

Go up in-to this moun-tain. Go up

Go up in-to this moun-tain. Go up

Go up in-to this moun-tain. Go

② und siehe das Land,
and see the land

in - to this moun - tain and see the land

in - to this moun - tain and see the land

up in - to this moun - tain and see the

Go up in - to this moun - tain and see the

③ das Ich Israel gegeben habe.
which I have given Israel.

S: the land. _ Go _____ up _

A: the land. _ Go _____ up _

T: giv-en Is - ra - el. Go up _ and see, see _ the land

B: giv-en Is - ra - el. Go up _ and see, see _ the land

(4) Und wenn du es gesehen hast,
And when you have seen it,

S: and see the land, _ and _____

A: and see the land, _ and _____

T: which I ___ have gi - ven Is - ra - el. And when ___ you have

B: which I ___ have gi - ven Is - ra - el. And when ___ you have

⑤ sollst du zu deinem Volk versammelt werden.
you shall be gather'd to your people.

74

S: you shall be gath-er'd to your, you shall be gath-er'd to your, you shall be gath-er'd to your

A: you shall be gath-er'd to your, you shall be gath-er'd to your, you shall be gath-er'd to your

T: gath - er'd to your peo- ple, peo-ple,

B: gath - er'd to your peo-ple, peo-ple,

77

S: you shall be gath-er'd to your peo - - ple.

A: you shall be gath-er'd to your peo - - ple.

T: peo-ple. You shall be gath-er'd to your peo - ple.

B: peo-ple. You shall be gath-er'd to your peo - ple.

⑥ Und ich flehte den Herrn an
And I besought the Lord

#2 Scene And I besought the Lord

Allegro Moderato

And I be-sought the Lord

⑦ zu jener Zeit und sprach,
at that time, saying,

⑧ O Herr Gott,
O Lord God,

at that time, say-ing, O, Lord, God.

O, Lord, God.

O, Lord, God.

⑨ Du hast deinem Diener angefangen
You have begun to show thy servant

13

Mos: You have be - gun to show thy ser - vant thy

T: You have be - gun to show thy ser - vant thy

B: You have be - gun to show thy ser - -

⑩ Deine Größe und deine mächtige Hand zu zeigen.
Thy greatness and thy mighty hand.

16

Mos: great-ness, and thy might y - hand.

T: great-ness,

B: vant thy great-ness,

mf

f

(11) Denn welcher Gott ist im Himmel oder auf Erden,
For what god is there, in heaven or in earth,

(12) der tun kann nach deinen Werken
that can do according to thy works

(13) und nach deiner Macht?
and according to thy might?

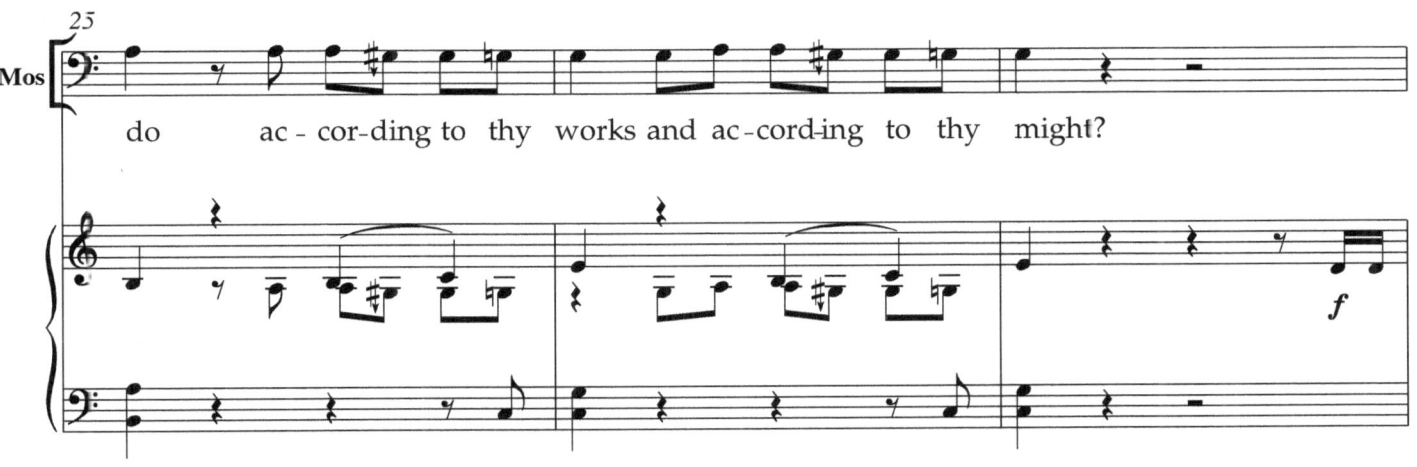

(14) Ich bitte dich, lass mich hinübergehen
I pray thee, let me go over

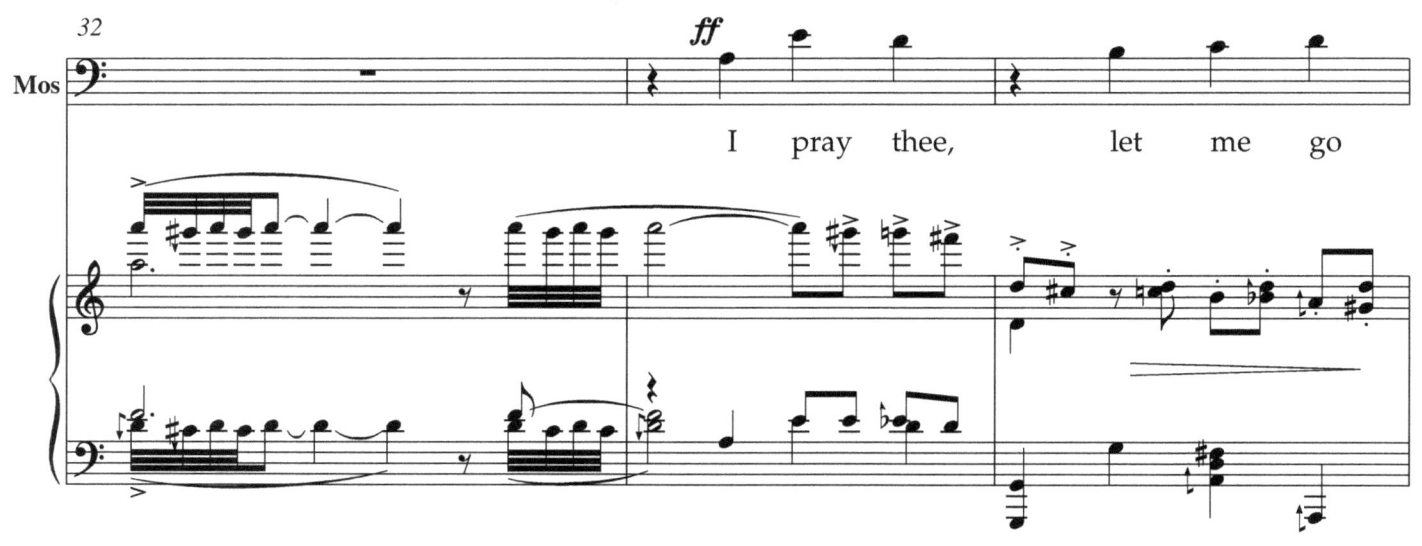

(15) und das gute Land sehen, das jenseits des Jordans liegt.
and see the good land that is beyond Jordan.

16 Du sollst nicht über den Jordan gehen.
Thou shalt not go over Jordan.

#3 Fugue Thou shalt not go

15
S
Jor - dan, o - ver Jor-dan. Thou shalt not go, shalt not
A
Jor - dan. Thou shalt not go o - ver Jor-dan.
T
o - ver Jor - - dan. Thou shalt not
B
Thou shalt not go o - ver Jor-dan.
20
go o - ver Jor - dan.
p
Thou shalt not, shalt not go
Thou shalt not, shalt not, shalt not go o - ver Jor - dan,
go o - ver Jor-dan.
Thou shalt not, shalt
(Fl.)
mf
p

S: o - ver Jor - dan. Thou shalt _ not, shalt _
A: Jor - dan. Thou shalt not go o - ver
T: Thou shalt. not go o - ver Jor - dan, o - ver
B: not, shalt. not go o - ver Jor - dan. Thou _

S: not, shalt _ not, shalt _ not, shalt _ not go _ o - ver,
A: Jor - dan, o - ver Jor - dan.
T: Jor - dan, Jor - - - - dan.
B: shalt _ not _ go o - ver

thou shalt not, shalt not, shalt not shalt not go _ o - ver Jor - dan.

Thou shalt not go o - ver Jor - dan.

Thou shalt not go o - ver Jor - dan.

Jor - dan. Thou shalt not go o - ver

Thou shalt not

Thou shalt not go o - ver Jor - dan.

Thou

Jor - dan, o - ver Jor - dan.

Lyrics:

S: not go o - ver. Thou _____ shalt not go,
A: not go o - ver Jor - dan o-ver Jor - dan.
T: Jor - dan, o - - ver

B: - - dan.

S: thou _____ shalt not go o - - - -
A: Jor - dan, Jor - dan, Jor - dan. Thou shalt
T: Jor - dan. O - ver Jor - dan, o-ver Jor - dan.

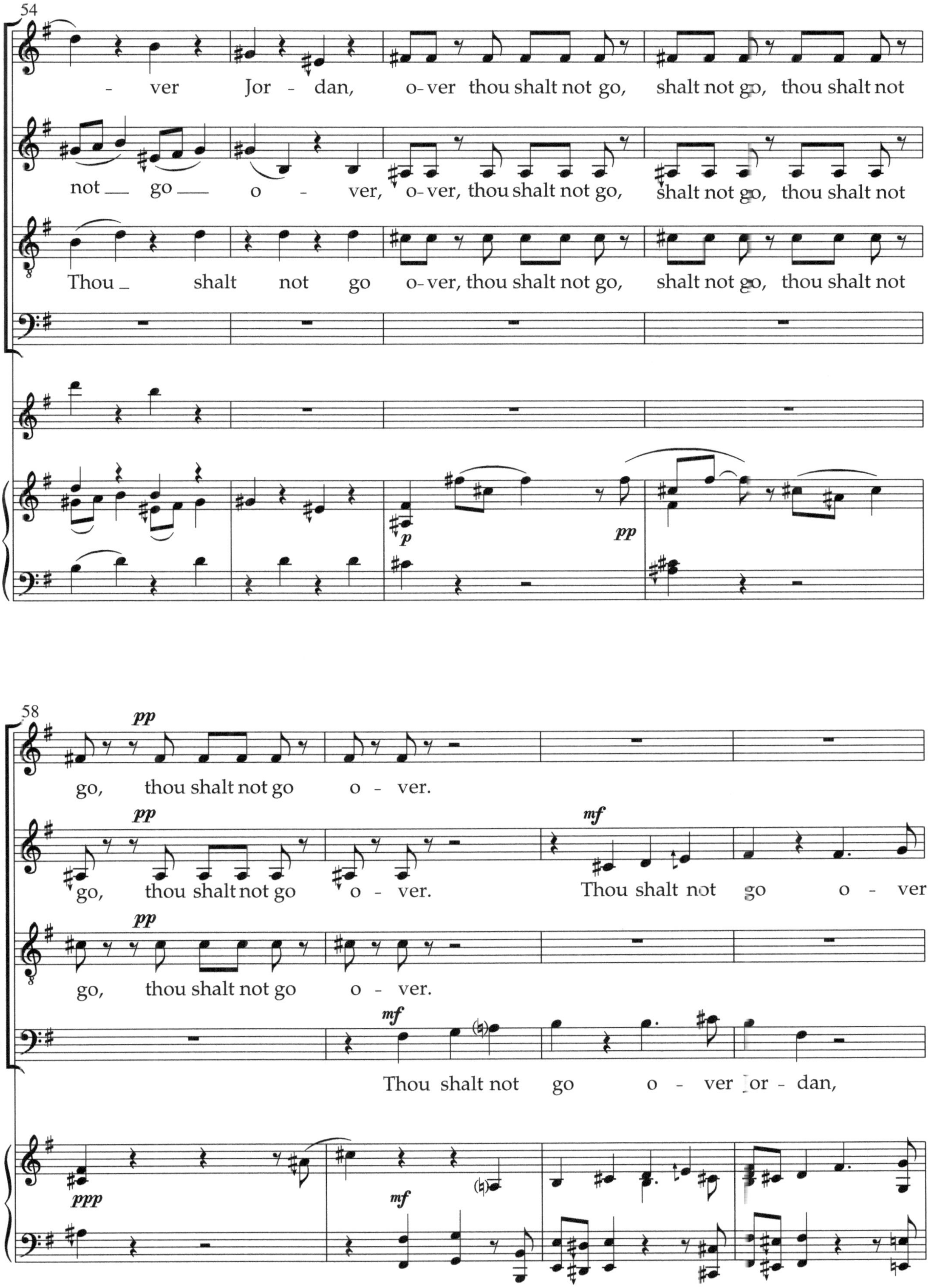

54

S: -ver Jor - dan, o-ver thou shalt not go, shalt not go, thou shalt not

A: not __ go __ o - ver, o-ver, thou shalt not go, shalt not go, thou shalt not

T: Thou __ shalt not go o-ver, thou shalt not go, shalt not go, thou shalt not

B:

58

S: go, thou shalt not go o - ver.

A: go, thou shalt not go o - ver. Thou shalt not go o - ver

T: go, thou shalt not go o - ver.

B: Thou shalt not go o - ver Jor - dan,

Thou shalt not go o - ver Jor - dan.

Shalt not,

Thou shalt not go o - ver

ver, o - ver Jor - dan, o - ver

thou shalt not go o - ver

Jor - dan.

Jor - dan. Thou shalt not go

(Tbn.)

S: Thou shalt not go o - ver Jor - dan, shalt not

A: Jor - dan, thou shalt not go, shalt not go, thou shalt not go, thou shalt not

T: Thou shalt not go o - ver

B: o - ver, thou shalt not go, shalt not go, thou shalt not go, not

S: go, shalt not go. Shalt not go o - ver Jor - dan.

A: go, thou shalt not go. Shalt not go o - ver Jor - dan.

T: Jor - dan, shalt not go. Shalt not go o - ver Jor - dan.

B: go,__ thou shalt not go. Shalt not go o - ver Jor - dan.

PART II. At the Side of the Wilderness: God called to him

#4 Recitative Now Moses kept the flocks

F♮ Moderato (♩=108-116)

Piano

(17) Moses hütete die Herde seines Schwiegervaters,
Now Moses kept the flocks of his father-in-law,

THE ECSTATIC

Now Mo - ses kept the flocks ___ of his

(18) des Priesters von Midian.
the priest of Midian,

(19) Und er trieb die Herde zur Seite der Wüste,
And he led the flock to the side of the wilderness,

fa - ther - in - law, the priest of Mi - dian, and

(20) und kam zum Berg Gottes.
and came to the mountain of God.

he led the flocks to the side of the wil-der-ness and came to the

moun-tain of ___ God.

#5 Aria And the angel of the Lord

Allegro moderato ($\quarternote$ =104-112)

The
Ecstatic

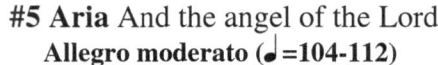

(21) Und der Engel des Herrn
And the angel of the Lord

(22) erschien ihm in einer Feuerflamme
appeared to him in a flame of fire

And the an-gel of the Lord ap - pear- ed to him in a flame of fire, in a

(23) aus der Mitte eines Busches,
out of the midst of a bush,

flame of fire, out of the midst of a bush, and he

(24) und er sah hin, und siehe!
And he looked, and lo!

(25) Der Busch brannte im Feuer.
the bush burned with fire.

looked, he looked and lo! the bush _____ burned with

fire, the bush burned with fire. And the an - - - - - - - gel of the Lord_____ ap - peared to him in a flame, a flame of

fire.

out of the midst of a

bush. He looked and lo! the

bush, the bush burned with

MOSES (falsetto)

the bush burned with

(26) Aber der Busch wurde nicht verzehrt.
But the bush was not consumed.

sumed. The bush burned with

The bush burned with

fire, but the bush was not con - sumed.

fire.

#6 Scene When the Lord saw

27 Als der Herr sah, dass Mose sich umwandte, um zu sehen,
When the Lord saw that Moses turned aside to see,

Lord saw that Mo-ses turned a - side _____ to see,

28 rief Gott ihm zu:
God called to him:

God called to him:

㉙ Mose, Mose.
Moses, Moses.

㉚ Und er sagte,
And he said,

㉛ Hier bin ich.
Here am I.

㉜ Ich bin der Gott deiner Väter,
I am the God of your fathers,

(33) der Gott Abrahams, der Gott Isaaks,
the God of Abraham, the God of Isaac,

(34) der Gott Jakobs.
the God of Jacob.

(35) Und Moses verbarg sein Gesicht,
And Moses hid his face

(36) denn er fürchtete sich, Gott anzuschauen.
for he was afraid to look at God.

(37) Ich habe des Elend
I have seen the affliction

(38) meines Volkes in Ägypten gesehen.
of my people who are in Egypt.

#7 Chorale I have seen the affliction of my people

A Movendo ($\quad$=ca 116)

(39) Ich bin gekommen, um sie
I have come to deliver them

(40) aus der Hand der Ägypter zu befreien.
out of the hand of the Egyptians.

40 aus der Hand der Ägypter zu befreien.
out of the hand of the Egyptians.

Scene Who am I?
#8 Caravanserai ($\quarternote$ =80-88)

Piano Reduction

41 Wer bin ich, dass ich die Söhne Israels
Who am I, that I should lead the sons of Israel

Mos: Who am I, that I should bring the sons of

S A: Ah,

42 aus Ägypten führen soll?
out of Egypt?

Mos: Is - ra - el out, Is - ra - el out of E - gypt?

S A: ah.

rit.

(43) Ich werde gewiss mit dir sein,
I will surely be with you,

(44) dies soll dir ein Zeichen sein:
for this shall be a token to you:

(45) Du wirst Gott auf diesem Berg dienen.
You shall serve God on this mountain.

(46) Wenn ich zu Israel komme und sage, der Gott eurer Väter
If I come to Israel and say, the God of you fathers

(47) hat mich zu euch gesandt?
has sent me to you?

(48) Und wenn sie mich fragen, wie ist sein Name?
And if they ask me, what is his name?

(49) Was soll ich ihnen sagen?
What should I tell them?

(50) Was soll ich zu ihnen sagen?
What should I say to them?

#9 Fugue Say this, I AM THAT I AM

Allegro Maestoso

51 Sage dies, ICH BIN, DER ICH BIN, 52 Sate dies zum Volk Israel.
Say this, I AM THAT I AM, Say this to the people of Israel.

53 Sage zum Volk Israel, ICH BIN.
Say to the people of Israel, I AM.

(54) ICH BIN der Herr, Gott Abrahams und Isaaks. (55) ICH BIN hat mich gesandt, sage ICH BIN DER ICH BIN.
I AM the Lord, God of Abraham and Isaac. I AM has sent me, say I AM THAT I AM.

A: Say to the peo-ple of Is - ra-el, I AM. I AM the Lord, God of

T: AM. I AM the Lord, God of

B: I AM the Lord, God of Is - ra-el, say I AM the Lord, God of

S: Say to the peo - ple of Is - ra - el, I AM.

A: A - bra-ham and I - saac. I AM has sent me, say I AM has sent me.

T: A - bra-ham. I AM, God of Is - ra - el, I

B: A - bra-ham.

S: I AM the Lord, God of A-bra-ham and I - saac.

A: I AM has sent me, has sent me.

T: AM, _____ I AM. _____ I _____

B: I AM has sent me, say

S: I _____ AM has sent me.

A: I AM has sent me, say I AM has sent me.

T: AM has sent me.

B: I AM has sent me.

Lyrics:
S: I AM has sent me to you. I AM, I AM, I AM, I AM.
A: I AM has sent me to you. I AM, I AM, I AM, I AM.
T: Say to the peo - ple of Is - ra - el,

(C♮ : ♮ Db = Db♮♮ : Db)

S: I AM, I AM the Lord, God of A-bra-ham and I - saac, I AM THAT I

A: saac. I AM THAT I AM, THAT I AM has sent me to__ you,

T: I AM THAT I AM, THAT I AM.

B: Lord, God of A - bra-ham and I - saac. I AM THAT___ I

S: AM.

A: has sent me to___ you. Say_____

T: The Lord your God_ has sent, has sent me

B: AM THAT___ I AM THAT___ I AM I

(56) Sage ICH BIN, der Herr, euer Gott.
Say I AM, the Lord, your God.

57 Oh, mein Herr, ich bin nicht beredt,
Oh, my Lord, I am not eloquent,

#10 Recitative Oh, my Lord
Lento

58 Nicht jetzt, nicht zuvor, un nicht seitdem
Not now, not before, and not since

59 Du zu deinem Diener gesprochen hast, 60 denn ich bin schwerfällig im Sprechen und in der Zunge.
Thou hast spoken to thy servant, for I am slow of speech and of tongue.

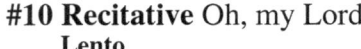

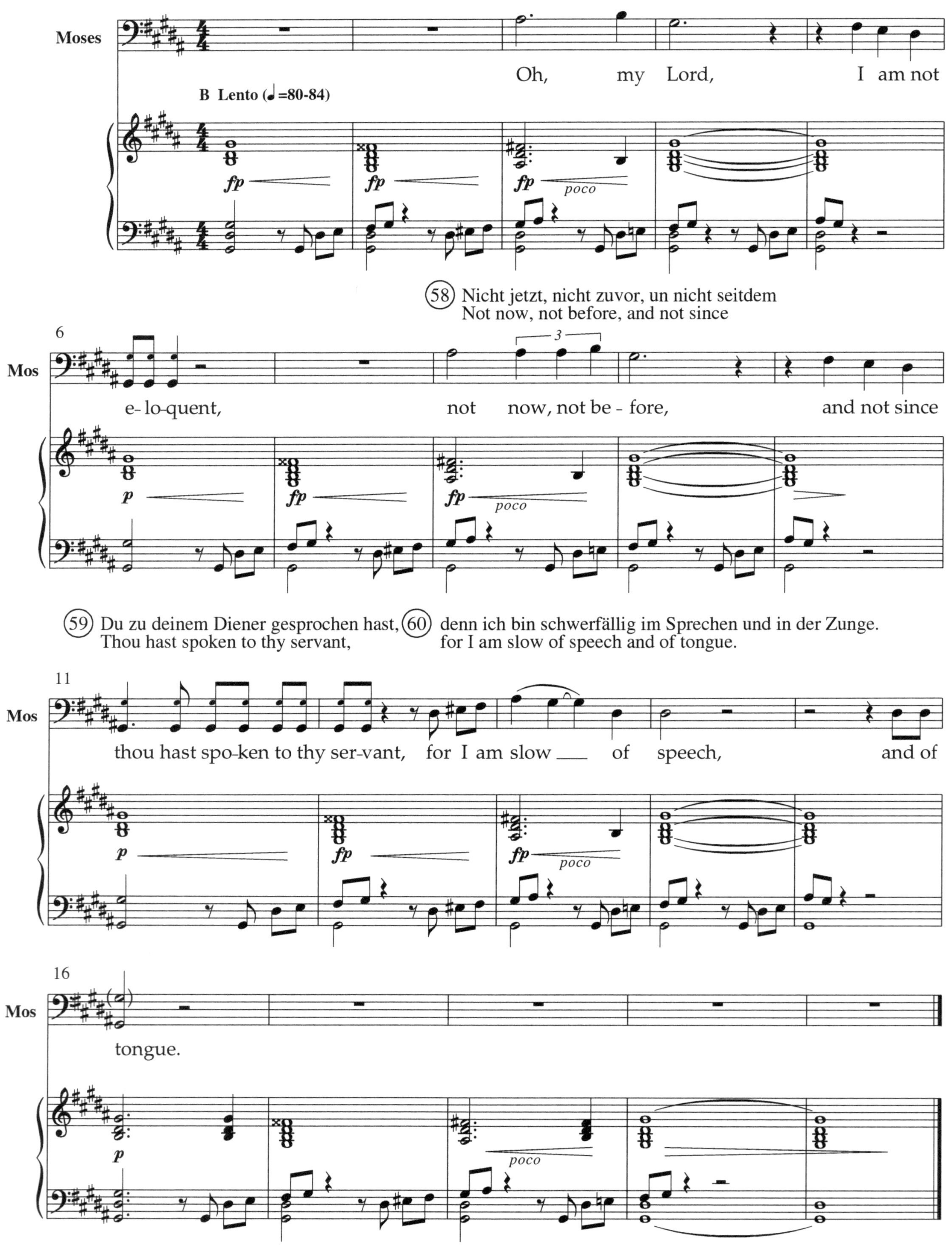

PART III. The Successes of Moses: How fair are your tents.

(61) Wie schön sind deine Zelte, Jakob,
How fair are your tents, O Jacob.

#11 Chorale How fair are your tents, O Jacob

F# Moderato ($\quarternote$ = 76-80)

(62) deine Wohnstätten, Israel.
your encampments, O Israel.

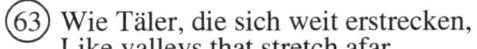

63 Wie Täler, die sich weit erstrecken,
Like valleys that stretch afar,

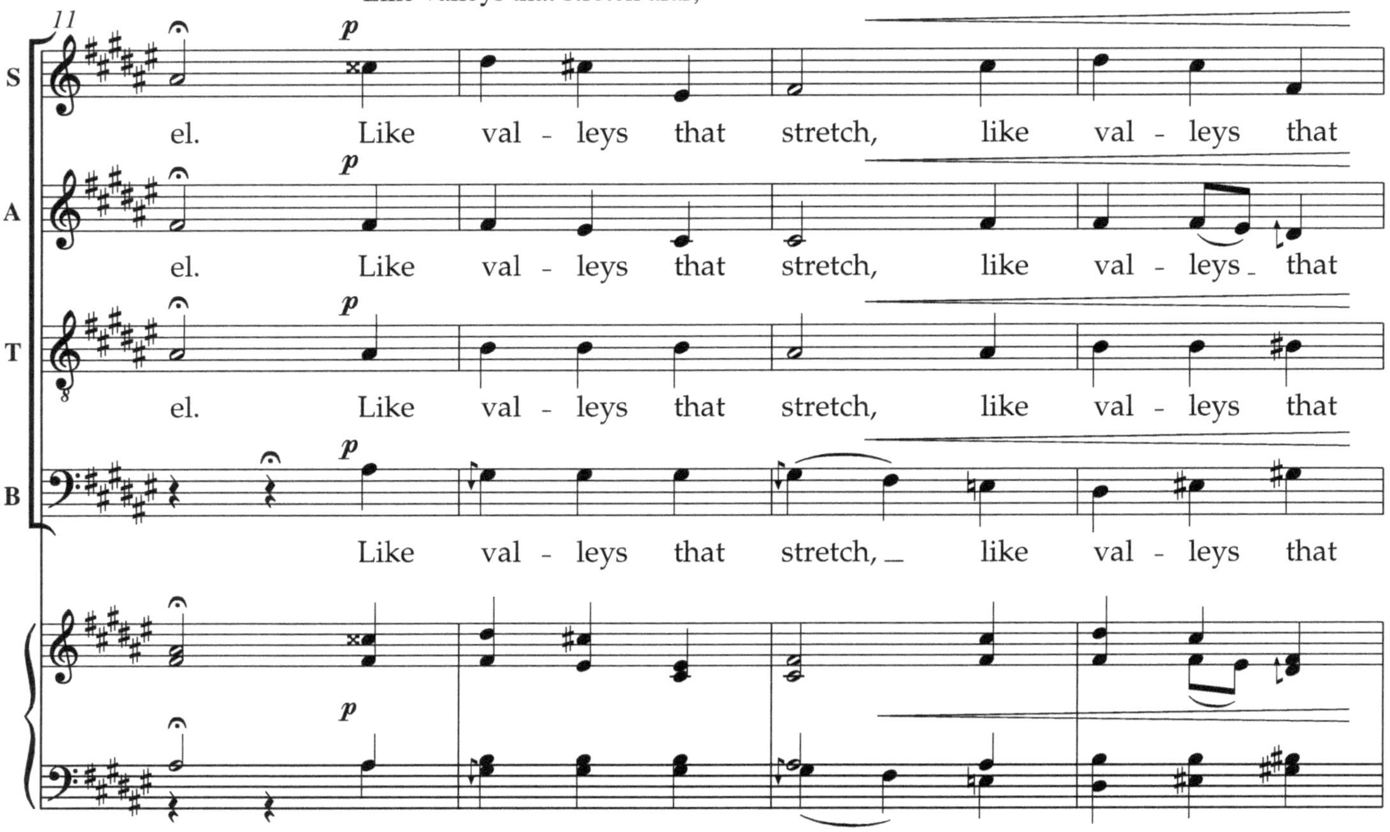

S: el. Like val - leys that stretch, like val - leys that

A: el. Like val - leys that stretch, like val - leys that

T: el. Like val - leys that stretch, like val - leys that

B: Like val - leys that stretch, like val - leys that

64 wie Gärten am Fluss.
like gardens beside a river.

a tempo

S: stretch a - far, like gar - dens be -

A: stretch a - far, like gar - dens be -

T: stretch a - far, like gar - dens be -

B: stretch a - far, be -

S: side a ri - ver. How fair are your tents, O Ja - cob, O

A: side a ri - ver. How fair are your tents, O Ja - cob, O

T: side a ri - ver. How fair are your tents, O Ja - cob, O

B: side a ri - ver. How fair are your tents, O Ja - cob,

S: Ja - cob. How fair are your tents, O Ja - cob.

A: Ja - cob. How fair are your tents, O Ja - cob.

T: Ja - cob. How fair are your tents, O Ja - cob.

B: How fair are your tents, O Ja - cob.

(65) Das Orakel Bileams, des Sohnes Beors.
The oracle of Balaam, son of Beor.

#12 Recitative The oracle of Balaam

The Ecstatic

(66) Das Orakel desjenigen, dessen Auge geöffnet ist.
The oracle of one whose eye is opened.

(67) Das Orakel dessen, der die Worte Gottes hört.
The oracle of one who hears the words of God.

(68) der die Vision des Allmächtigen sieht,
who sees the vision of the Almighty,

(69) niederfallend, aber mit unverhüllten Augen.
falling down, but having eyes uncovered.

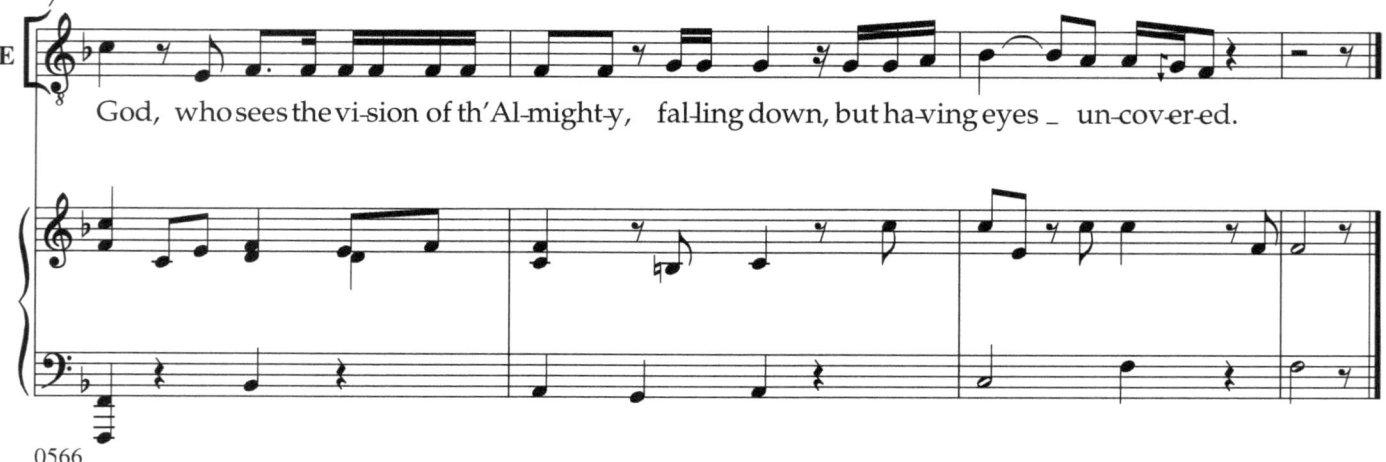

#13 Chorus He has not beheld misfortune in Jacob

70 Er hat kein Unglück in Jakob gesehen,
He has not beheld misfortune in Jacob,

He has not be-held mis-for-tune, mis-for-tune in

71 noch hat er Leid in Israel erblickt.
nor has he seen trouble in Israel.

Ja - cob   nor has he seen trou-ble,   seen

He has not be-held mis-for-tune in   Ja - cob

0566

trou - ble in Is - ra - el.

nor has he seen trou-ble in Is - ra - el.

The

(72) Der Herr, ihr Gott, ist mit ihnen,
The Lord their God is with them.

(73) Und der Ruf eines Königs ist unter ihnen.
And the shout of a king is among them.

Lord their God is with them, and the shout ___ of a king is a-

(D: G = G: G)

(74) Denn von der Spitze der Berge sehe ich ihn,
For from the top of a mountain I see him.

mong them. For from the top of the moun - tain, from the

Ww.

(75) von den Hügeln schaue ich ihn.
from the hills I behold him.

54

(76) Siehe, ein Volk, das für sich wohnt,
Lo, a people dwelling alone,

32

E
Lo! a peo - ple, dwell - ing a - lone,

S
Lo! a peo - ple, dwell - ing a - lone,

A
Lo! a peo - ple, dwell - ing a - lone,

(Fl)
mf p

p

(77) und sich nicht zu den Nationen zählt.
not reckoning itself among the nations.

36

E
lo, a peo - ple dwel - ling a - lone, ___ not rec-kon-ing it - self a - mong the

S
lo, a peo - ple dwel - ling a - lone, not rec-kon-ing it - self a - mong the

A
lo, a peo - ple dwel - ling a - lone, not rec-kon-ing it - self a - mong the

0566

(78) Wer kann den Staub Jakobs zählen?
who can count the dust of Jacob?

na - tions, who can count the dust of Ja - cob, who can count the dust of Ja - cob?

na - tions,

na - tions,

rit.

Who can count the dust of

Who can count the dust of Ja - cob?

Who can count the dust of Ja - cob?

(79) Wie eine Löwin erhebt es sich.
Like a lioness it rises up,

Ja - cob?

Like a li - on - ess,

like a

a tempo

48

E: li - on-ess, it ri - - - - -

(80) und wie ein Löwe erhebt es sich,
and like a lion it lifts itself,

50

E: - ses up.

S: And like a lion, and

A: And like a lion, and

(Tbn)

(81) es legt sich nicht nieder, bis es die Beute gefressen
it does not lie down, till it devours the prey

53

S: like a lion it lifts it - self, it does not lie down, till it de-

A: like a lion it lifts it - self, it does not lie down, till it de-

(Vla, Ww.)

(82) und das Blut der Erschlagenen getrunken hat.
and drinks the blood of the slain.

vours,__ till it de- vours the prey and

vours,__ till it de- vours the prey and

He has not be-held mis-

drinks the blood of the slain.

drinks the blood of the slain.

for-tune, mis-for-tune in Ja-cob

He has not be-held mis-for-tune in Ja-cob

nor has he seen trou-ble, seen trou-ble in Is-ra-el.

nor has he seen trou-ble in

Is-ra-el.

The Lord their God is with them, and the shout __ of a king is a-

Lyrics:

(S) For from the top of the moun-tain, from the
(A) mong them. For from the top of the moun-tain, from the

(S) top _ of the moun-tain I see him, from the hills _____ I be-hold him, _____
(A) top _ of the moun-tain I see him, from the hills _____ I be-hold him, _____

Lyrics: I be - hold him. / I be - hold him. / Lo! a peo - ple, dwel - ling a- / lone, lo, a peo - ple dwel - ling a - lone, ___ not

rec-kon-ing it - self a - mong the na - tions, who can count the dust of Ja - cob, who can

count the dust of Ja - cob?

Who can count the dust of Ja - cob?

Who can count the dust of Ja - cob?

(83) Dann zog Sihon mit all seinem Volk aus,
Then Sihon came out against them,

#14 Recitative Then Sihon came out

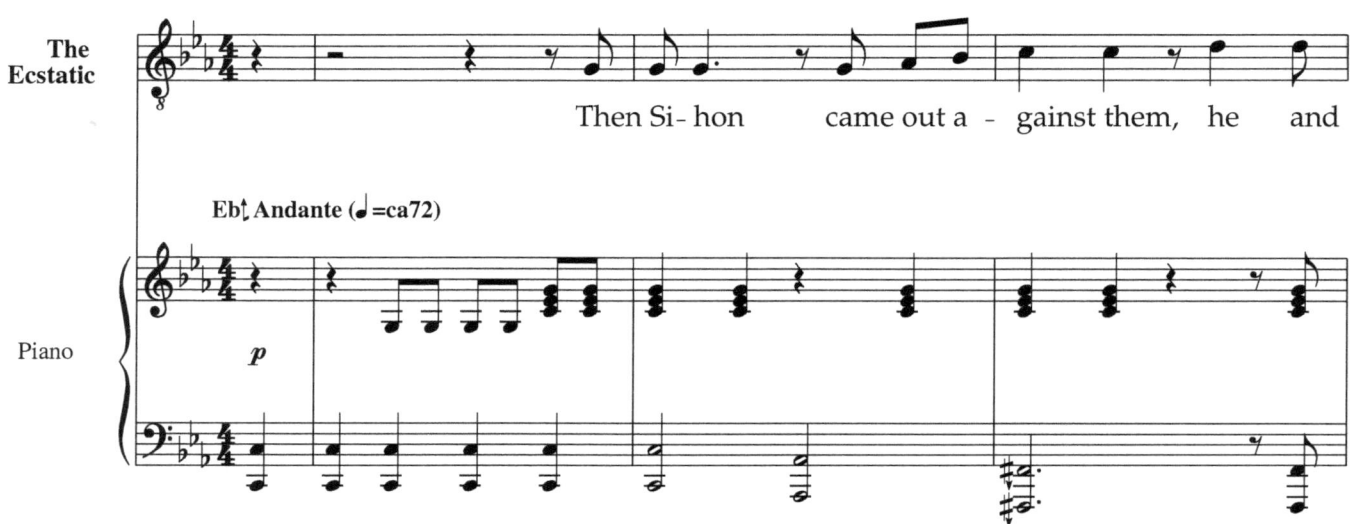

The Ecstatic: Then Si- hon came out a - gainst them, he and

Eb: Andante ($\quarternote$=ca72)

Piano p

(84) um bei Jahaz zu kämpfen.
he and all his people, to fight at Jahaz.

E: all his peo - ple, to fight at Ja - haz.

#15 Chorus And the Lord delivered him

(85) Und der Herr, unser Gott, gab ihn uns preis.
And the Lord our God delivered him before us.

And the Lord our God de -

And the Lord our God de -

86) Und wir schlugen ihn, seine Söhne und all sein Volk.
And we smote him, and his sons, and all his people.

liv - - er'd him be - fore us. And we

smote him, and his sons, and all his

(87) Und wir nahmen zu der Zeit alle seine Städte ein.
And we took all his cities at that time.

(88) Und wir vernichteten die Männer,
And we utterly destroyed the men,

0566

(89) vernichteten die Frauen,
utterly destroyed the women,

(90) vernichteten die kleinen Kinder,
utterly destroyed the little children,

(91) wir ließen keinen übrig.
we left none to remain.

S: fore us, and we smote him, and his

A: fore us, and we smote him, and his

T: none, none to re - main. We smote him and his

B: none, none to re - main. We smote him and his

S: sons and all his peo - ple. And we took all his

A: sons and all his peo - ple. And we took all his

T: sons and all his peo - ple. And we took all his

B: sons and all his peo - ple.

S: ci - ties, and we took all his ci - ties at that time, that time, that

A: ci - ties, and we took all his ci - ties at that time, that time, that

T: ci - ties, and we took all his ci - ties at that time, that time, that

S: time. And we ut - ter - ly des - troy'd the men and the wo - men and the

A: time. And we ut - ter - ly des - troy'd the men and the wo - men and the

T: time. And we ut - ter - ly des - troy'd the men and the wo - men and the

B: And the Lord our

S: lit-tle chil-dren, we left none, the men and the wo-men and the lit-tle chil-dren we left none to re-

A: lit-tle chil-dren, we left none, the men and the wo-men and the lit-tle chil-dren we left none to re-

T: lit-tle chil-dren, we left none, the men and the wo-men and the lit-tle chil-dren we left none to re-

B: God de-li - - ver'd him be -

S: main. And we smote him and his

A: main. And we smote him and his

T: main. And we smote him and his

B: fore us. And we smote him and his

S: sons — and all his peo-ple. And we ut-ter-ly des-troy'd the
A: sons — and all his peo-ple. And we ut-ter-ly des-troy'd the
T: sons — and all his peo-ple. And we ut-ter-ly des-troy'd the
B: sons — And the

S: men and the wo-men and the lit-tle chil-dren we left none, the men and the wo-men and the
A: men and the wo-men and the lit-tle chil-dren we left none, the men and the wo-men and the
T: men and the wo-men and the lit-tle chil-dren we left none, the men and the wo-men and the
B: Lord our God de - li - - - ver'd

S: lit - tle chil - dren we left none to re - main.

A: lit - tle chil - dren we left none to re - main.

T: lit - tle chil - dren we left none to re - main.

B: him be - fore us.

S: And we smote him and his sons

A: And we smote him and his sons

T: And we smote him and his sons

B: And we smote him and his sons

and all his peo - ple, we left none to re - main.

and all his peo - ple, we left none to re - main.

and all his peo - ple, we left none. And the

and all his peo - ple, we left none. And the

Lord our God de - li - ver'd

Lord our God de - li - ver'd

and all his peo - ple.

and all his peo - ple.

and all his peo - ple.

and all his peo - ple.

fff

92 Dann zog Og, der König von Baschan, gegen sie aus,
Then Og the King of Bashan came out against them,

#16 Recitative Then Og the King of Bashan came out

93 er und all sein Volk, zum Kampf bei Edrei.
he and all his people, to battle at Edrei.

94 aber der Herr sprach zu Mose:
but the Lord said to Moses:

#17 Chorale Do not fear him.

95 Fürchte ihn nicht,
Do not fear him,

76

(96) denn ich habe ihn in deine Hand gegeben.
for I have given him into your hand.

PART IV. The Laws: Surely this great nation

(97) Siehe, ich habe euch Gesetze un Rechtsprechungen gelehrt,
Behold, I have taught you statutes and judgments.

#18 Recitative Behold I have taught you

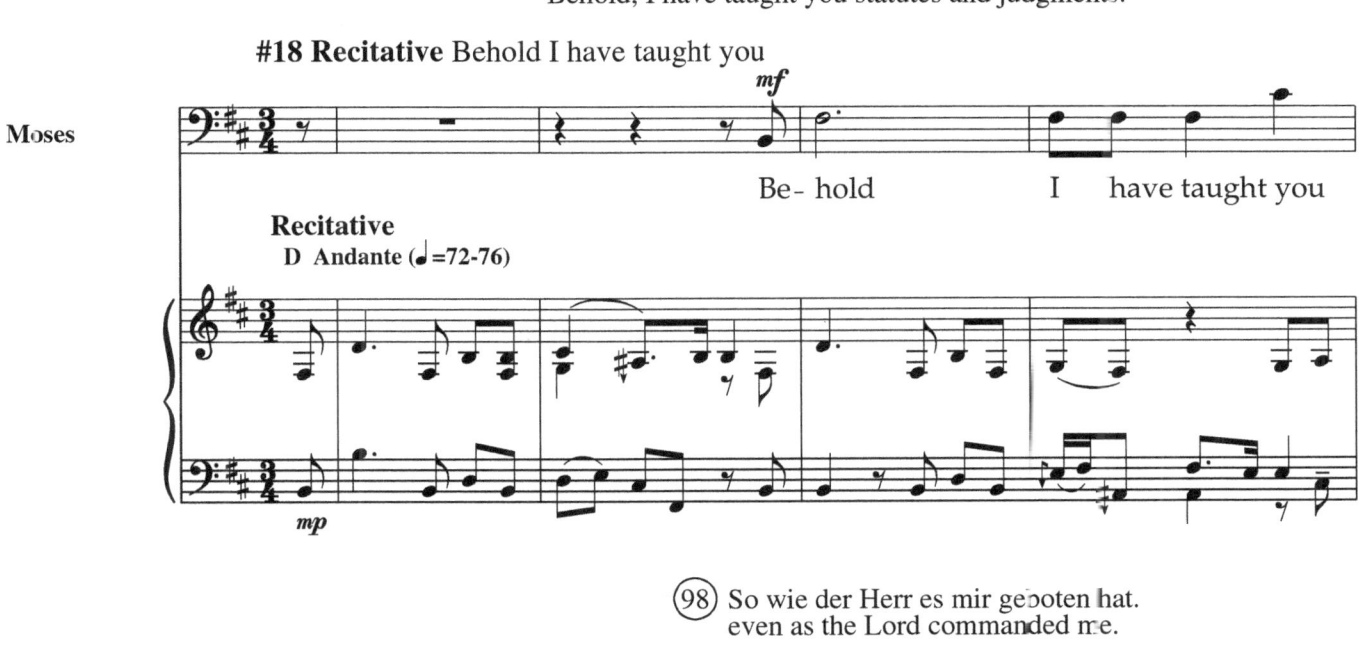

(98) So wie der Herr es mir geboten hat.
even as the Lord commanded me.

#19 Canon Thou Shalt Have No Other God

Du sollst keine anderen Götter neben mir haben.
Thou shalt have no other god before me.

shalt _____ have no oth-er god be-fore _____ me.

Thou shalt _____ have no oth-er god be-fore _____ me.

100 Du sollst dir kein geschnitztes Bildnis machen
Thou shalt not make unto thee a graven image.

(101) oder irgendein Abbild von irgendetwas, das im Himmel oben
or any likeness of any living thing in heaven

(102) oder auf der Erde oder im Wasser ist;
or on earth or in the water;

(103) du sollst dich vor ihnen nicht niederwerfen und sie nicht dienen.
thou shalt not bow down to them and serve them.

(104) Du sollst den Namen des Herrn deines Gottes nicht missbrauchen.
Thou shalt not take the name of the Lord thy God in vain.

(105) Gedenke des Sabbattages, um ihn heilig zu halten.
Remember the Sabbath day to keep it holy.

(106) Ehre deinen Vater und deine Mutter.
Honor thy father and mother.

(107) Du sollst nicht töten.
Thou shalt not kill.

(108) Du sollst nicht stehlen.
Thou shalt not steal.
(109) Du sollst nicht ehebrechen.
Thou shalt not commit adultery.

40
S
Thou shalt not kill. Thou shalt not
A
T
fa - ther and mo - ther. Thou shalt not steal.
B
Thou shalt not com-
(Fl.)

(110) Du sollst kein fasches Zeugnis ablegen gegen deinen Nächsten.
Thou shalt not bear false witness against thy neighbor.

46
S
steal.
A
Thou shalt not com-mit a - dul-ter-y.
T
Thou shalt not
B
mit a-dul-ter-y. Thou shalt not
(Tp.)

(111) Du sollst nicht begehren deines Nächsten Hab und Gut.
Thou shalt not covet anything that is thy neighbor's.

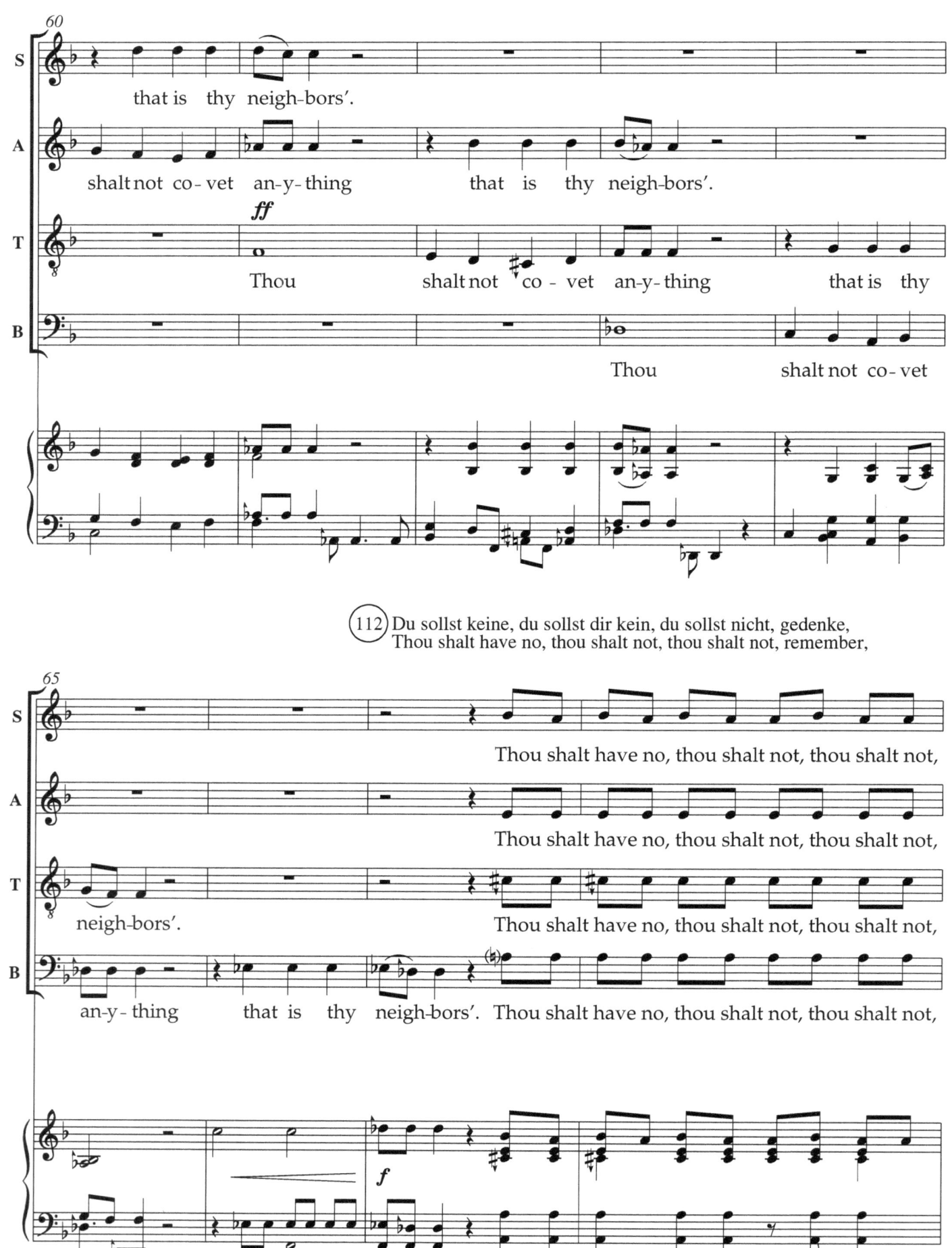

S: that is thy neigh-bors'.

A: shalt not co-vet an-y-thing that is thy neigh-bors'.

T: *ff* Thou shalt not co-vet an-y-thing that is thy

B: Thou shalt not co-vet

(112) Du sollst keine, du sollst dir kein, du sollst nicht, gedenke,
Thou shalt have no, thou shalt not, thou shalt not, remember,

S: Thou shalt have no, thou shalt not, thou shalt not,

A: Thou shalt have no, thou shalt not, thou shalt not,

T: neigh-bors'. Thou shalt have no, thou shalt not, thou shalt not,

B: an-y-thing that is thy neigh-bors'. Thou shalt have no, thou shalt not, thou shalt not,

(113) Ehre, dul sollst nicht du sollst nicht du sollst nicht du sollst nicht du sollst nicht.
honor, thou shalt not, thou shalt not, thou shalt not, thou shalt not, thou shalt not.

S: re - mem - ber, hon-or, thou shalt not, thou shalt not, thou shalt not, thou

A: re - mem - ber, hon-or, thou shalt not, thou shalt not, thou shalt not, thou

T: re - mem - ber, hon-or, thou shalt not, thou shalt not, thou shalt not, thou

B: re - mem - ber, hon-or, thou shalt not, thou shalt not, thou shalt not, thou

S: shalt not, thou shalt not.

A: shalt not, thou shalt not.

T: shalt not, thou shalt not.

B: shalt not, thou shalt not.

(114) Halte sie daher und tue sie,
Keep therefore and do them,

(115) denn das ist eure Weisheit und euer Verständnis
for this is your wisdom and your understanding

#20 Recitative Keep Therefore and Do Them

(116) in den Augen der Völker,
in the sight of the nations,

(117) die all diese Gesetze hören und sagen werden:
which shall hear all these statues and say:

(118) Wahrlich, diese große Nation ist ein weises und verständiges Volk.
Surely this great nation is a wise and understanding people.

#21 Chorus Surely this great nation
Allegro Moderato

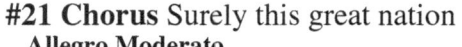

Sure - ly, sure - ly,

Sure - ly, sure - ly,

Sure - ly, sure - ly,

Sure-ly this great na-tion is a __ wise and un-der-stan-ding peo-ple. __

#21 Chorus
D Allegro Moderato (♩=108-116)

Orchestra Reduction

sure - ly, sure - ly.

sure - ly, sure - ly.

sure - ly, sure - ly.

sure-ly this great na-tion is a __ wise and un-der-stand-ing peo-ple. __

(D: ↕ F = ↕ F: F)

(119) denn welche Nation ist so groß,
For what nation is there so great,

(120) dass sie Götter so nahe bei sich hat wie der Herr?
who hath God so nigh unto them as the Lord.

For what na-tion is there __ so great, who hath God so nigh __ un-to them as the

For what na-tion is there __ so great, who hath God so nigh un-to them as the

(F♮ : ♮ Db = Db♯♯ : Db)

mf

Lord. Sure — ly, sure — — —

Lord. Sure — ly, sure — — —

Sure — ly, sure — — —

Sure-ly this great na-tion is a __ wise and un-der-stand-ing

(Db♯♯ : ♭ G = G: G)

f

0566

(121) Lehre deine Kinder, lehre dieses Gesetz deinen Kindern.
Teach your children, teach this law to your children.

(122) Lehre es den Kindern deiner Kinder.
Teach it to your children's children.

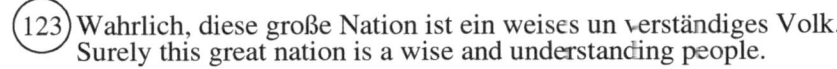

Teach this law, to your chil-dren. Teach this

Teach it to your chil-dren's chil-dren.

Teach it to your chil-dren's chil-dren.

Teach it to your chil-dren's chil-dren.

f (non troppo)

(123) Wahrlich, diese große Nation ist ein weises und verständiges Volk.
Surely this great nation is a wise and understanding people.

law to your chil-dren. Sure - - ly,

Teach this law to your chil-dren, teach it to your chil-dren. Sure-ly,

Teach this law to your chil-den. Sure - ly, sure-ly,

Teach this law to your chil-dren. Sure, _____ sure - ly, a

33

wise and un-der-stand-ing peo-ple. Sure, _____ sure - ly a

wise and un-der-stand-ing peo-ple. Sure, _____

wise and un-der-stand-ing peo-ple. Sure, _____

wise and un-der-stand-ing peo-ple. Sure, _____ sure - ly a

(D: ♮F = F♮ : F)

124 Welche große Nation hat so gerechte Satzungen und Regeln
What great nation has statutes and rules

37

wise and un-der-stand-ing peo - ple.

wise and un-der-stand-ing peo - ple.

wise and un-der-stand-ing peo - ple. What great na - tion has stat - utes and rules so

wise and un-der-stand-ing peo - ple. What great na - tion has stat - utes and rules so

(F♮ : ♮Ab = Ab♮♮ : Ab)

125 wie dieses ganze Gesetz? 126 Welche Nation hat Götter so nahe bei sich wie der Herr bei euch ist?
so righteous as all this law? What nation has God so nigh as the Lord is unto you?

0566

(127) Gib acht auf dich selbst und bewahre deine Seele sorgfältig.
Take heed to yourself and keep your soul closely.

chil-dren's chil-dren, teach it to your chil-dren. Take heed to your-

self and keep your soul close-ly, close-ly! Take heed to your-

128 Lehre dieses Gesetz, lehre deinen Kindern.
Teach this law, teach your children.

57

self and keep your soul close-ly. Teach this

self and keep your soul close-ly. Teach this

self and keep your soul close-ly. Teach this

Teach this

61

law, teach this law. Teach your chil - dren,

law, teach this law. Teach your chil - dren,

law, teach this law. Teach your chil - dren,

law, teach, teach this law. Teach your chil - dren,

129 Lehre den Kindern deiner Kinder.
Teach your children's children.

130 Lehre deine Kinder, lehre dieses Gesetz.
Teach your children, teach this law.

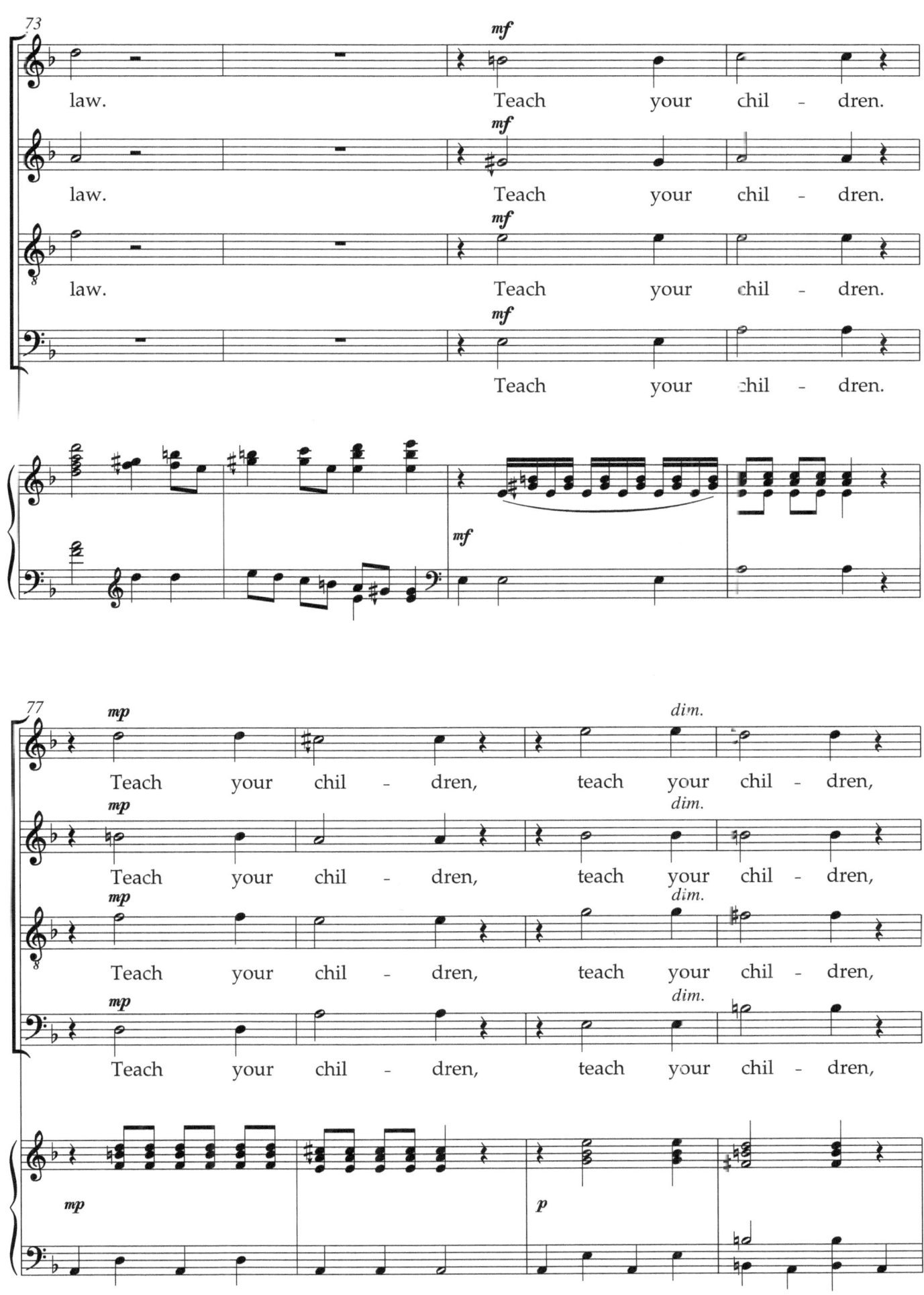

law. Teach your chil - dren.

Teach your chil - dren, teach your chil - dren,

teach your chil - dren, teach this law.

teach your chil - dren, teach this law.

teach your chil - dren, teach this law.

teach your chil - dren, teach this law.

Sure-ly this great na - tion is a wise and un-der-stand-ing peo - ple.

Sure-ly this great na - tion is a wise and un-der-stand-ing peo - ple.

Sure-ly this great na - tion is a wise and un-der-stand-ing peo - ple.

Sure-ly this great na - tion is a wise and un-der-stand-ing peo - ple.

Sure-ly this great na - tion is a wise and un-der-stand-ing peo-ple. ___

Sure-ly this great na - tion is a wise and un-der-stand-ing peo-ple. ___

Sure-ly this great na - tion is a wise and un-der-stand-ing peo-ple. ___

Sure-ly this great na - tion is a wise and un-der-stand-ing peo-ple. ___

(D: ♮ F = F♮: F)

For what na-tion is there ___ so great, who hath God so nigh un-to them as the

For what na-tion is there ___ so great, who hath God so nigh un-to them as the

(F♮: ♮ Db = Db♮♮: Db)

0566

Lord. Sure - ly, sure - ly.

Lord. Sure - ly, sure - ly.

Sure - ly, sure - ly.

Sure-ly this great na-tion is a __ wise and un-der-stand-ing peo-ple. __

(Db ♯♯ : ♩ G = G: G)

Teach, ____ teach ____ your chil-dren. Teach, ____ teach

Teach, ____ teach ____ your chil-dren. Teach, ____ teach

Teach ____ your chil-dren, teach, ____ your chil-dren. Teach ____ your chil-dren,

Teach, ____ teach ____ your chil-dren. Teach, ____ teach

(G: D = D: D)

your chil-dren.

your chil-dren. Teach it to your

teach, your chil-dren. Teach this law to your chil-dren. Teach it to your

your chil-dren. Teach this law. Teach it to your

Teach this law to your chil-dren. Sure-ly this great

chil-dren's chil-dren. Teach this law, teach it to your chil-dren. Sure-ly this great

chil-dren's chil-dren. Teach this law to your chil-dren. Sure-ly this great

chil-dren's chil-dren. Teach this law. Sure-ly this great

na - - tion, sure - ly this great na - tion,

na - - tion, sure - ly this great na - tion,

na - tion, sure - ly sure - ly this great na - - tion,

na - tion, sure - ly sure - ly this great na - tion,

sure - ly this great na - tion is a wise and un - der - stand - ing peo - ple.

sure - ly this great na - tion is a wise and un - der - stand - ing peo - ple.

sure - ly this great wise and un - der - stand - ing peo - ple.

sure - ly this great na - tion is _ a wise and un - der - stand - ing peo - ple.

Teach, teach this law to your chil - - d-en, teach,

Teach, teach this law to your chil - - d-en, teach,

Teach, teach this law to your chil - - d-en,

Teach, teach this law to your chil - - dren,

teach this law, this law.

teach this law, this law.

teach this law, this law.

teach this law, this law.

131

Teach this law, this

Teach this law, this

Teach this law, this

Teach this law, this

135

law.

law.

law.

law.

PART V. The Troubles: They weep unto me, thy people

#22 Rondo The Lord look upon you and judge

F♮ Allegro Moderato (♩.= 72-80)

Orchestra Reduction

① Der Herr shaue auf euch un richte.
The Lord look upon you and judge.

The Lord look up-on you and

The Lord look up-on you and

② Was habt ihr uns nun angetan?
What have you done to us now?

③ Ihn habt uns zu einem Ärgernis gemacht.
You made of us an offense

④ im Auge des Pharaos.
in the eye of the Pharaoh.

⑤ Was sollen wir essen? Was sollen wir trinken?
What shall we eat? What shall we drink?

judge. What have you done to us now? You made of us an of-

judge. What have you done to us now? You made of us an of-

Lord look up-on you and judge. What have you done to us now?

Lord look up-on you and judge. What have you done to us now?

fense in the eye of the Pha - - raoh. What shall we

fense in the eye of the Pha - - raoh. What shall we eat?

You made of us an of - fense in the eye of the Pha - raoh. What shall we eat?

You made of us an of - fense in the eye of the Pha - raoh. What shall we

0566

(6) Hätten wir doch durch die Hand des Herrn gestorben
Would we had died by the hand of the Lord

S: eat? What shall we eat? What shall we drink? Would we had died by the

A: What shall we eat? What shall we drink, drink? Would we had died by the

T: What shall we eat? What shall we drink, drink? Would we had died by the

B: eat? What shall we eat? What shall we drink? Would we had died by the

(7) im Land Ägypten. Hätten wir doch gestorben!
in the land of Egypt. Would we had died!

S: hand of the Lord in the land of E - gypt. Would we had died!

A: hand of the Lord in the land of E - gypt. Would we had died!

T: hand of the Lord in the land of E - gypt. Would we had died!

B: hand of the Lord in the land of E - gypt. Would we had died!

(Ww.)

(8) Der Herr schaue auf euch und richte.
The Lord look upon you and judge.

35

S: Would we had died! ... The Lord look up-on you and

A: Would we had died! ... The Lord look up-on you and

T: Would we had died!

B: Would we had died!

(9) Was habt ihr uns nun angetan?
What have you done to us now?

(10) Ihr habt uns zu Ärgernis gemacht
You made of us an offense

39

S: judge. What have you done to us now? _____ You made of us an of-

A: judge. What have you done to us now? You made of us an of-

T: Lord look up-on you and judge. What have you done to us now?

B: Lord look up-on you and judge. What have you done to us now?

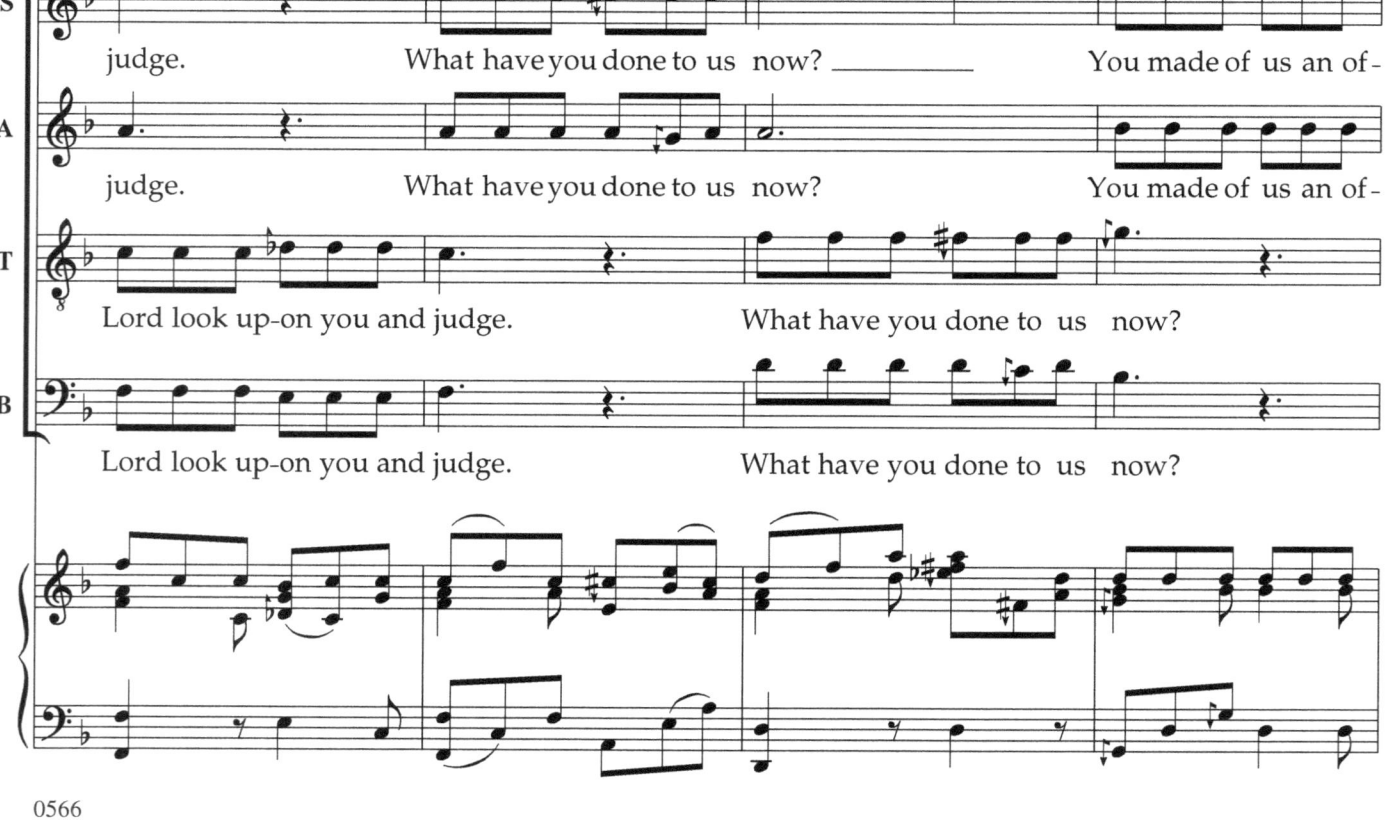

(11) im Auge des Pharaos.
in the eye of the Pharaoh.

43

S: fense in the eye of the Pha - - - raoh. _____

A: fense in the eye of the Pha - - - raoh. _____

T: You made of us an of - fense in the eye of the Pha - raoh.

B: You made of us an of - fense in the eye of the Pha - raoh.

(12) Hätten wir doch neben den Fleischtöpfen sterben dürfen, (13) wir saßen da und aßen uns satt
Would we had died by the side of the fleshpots, we sat there and ate to the full.

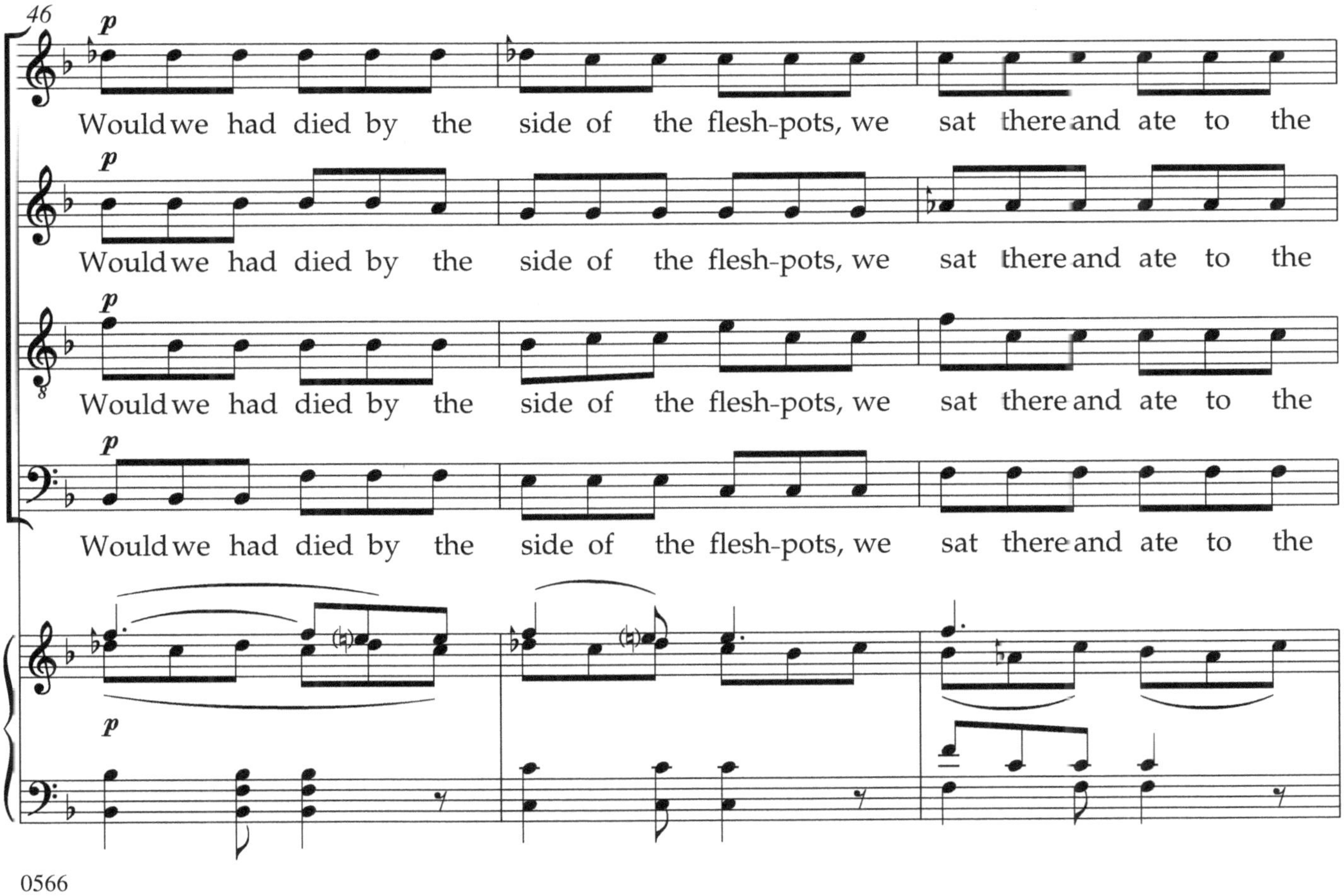

46 *p*

S: Would we had died by the side of the flesh-pots, we sat there and ate to the

A: Would we had died by the side of the flesh-pots, we sat there and ate to the

T: Would we had died by the side of the flesh-pots, we sat there and ate to the

B: Would we had died by the side of the flesh-pots, we sat there and ate to the

(14) Hätten wir doch gestorben!
Would we had died!

(15) Was sollen wir trinken? Hätten wir doch gestorben!
What shall we drink? Would we had died.

(16) Der Herr schaue auf euch und richte.
The Lord look upon you and judge.

(17) Was habt ihr uns nun angetan?
What have you done to us now?

(18) Nun ist unsere Kraft dahin
Now our strength is gone

(19) es gibt nichts außer diesem Manna.
there is nothing at all but this manna.

(20) Nun ist unsere Kraft dahin
Now our strength is gone

(21) es gibt nichts,
there is nothing,

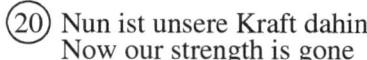

man - na. Now our strength is gone there is no- thing,

(22) nichts außer diesem Manna.
nothing at all but this manna.

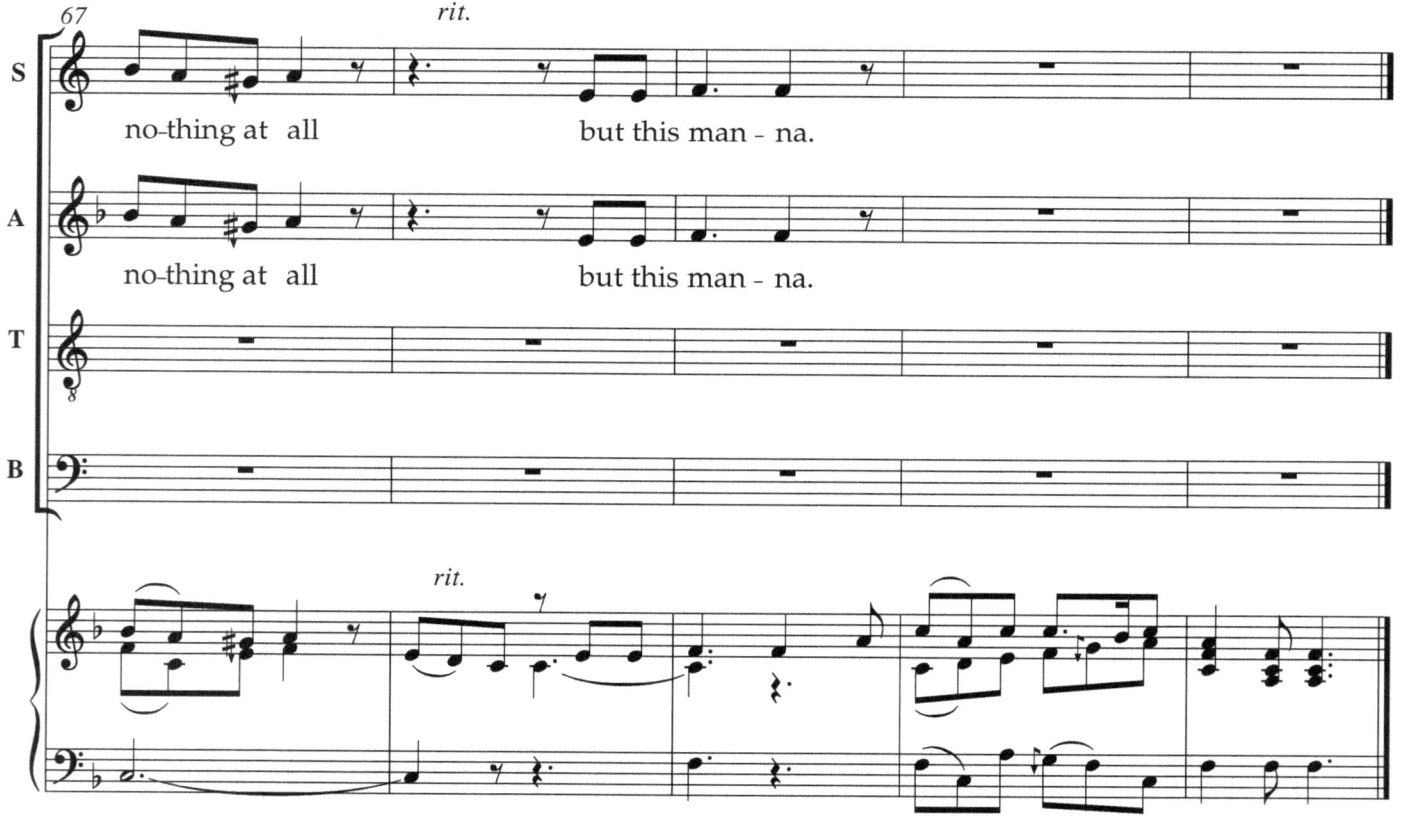

no-thing at all but this man - na.

(23) Warum hast du deinem Knecht so übel getan?
Why hast thou dealt ill with thy servant?

#23 Plaint Why hast thou dealt ill

Lento

(24) Warum habe ich keine Gnade gefunden in deinen Augen?
Why have I not found favor in thy sight?

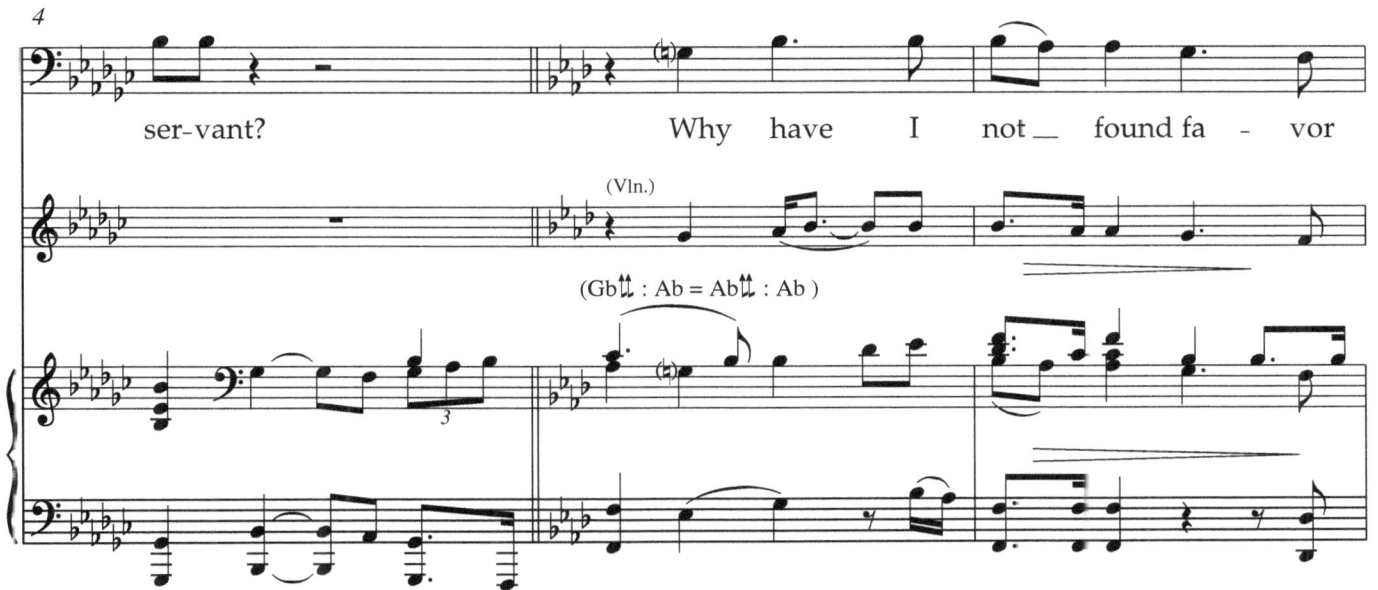

(25) dass du legst
that thou dost lay

0566

(26) die Last dieses ganzen Volkes auf mich legst.
the burden of all this people upon me.

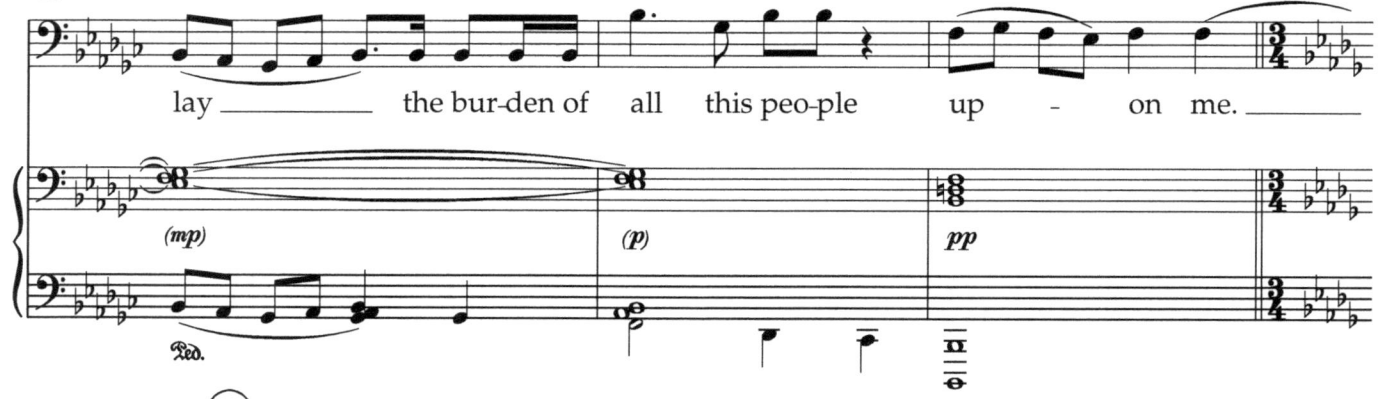

lay _____ the bur-den of all this peo-ple up - on me. _____

(mp)   (p)   pp

Ped.

(27) Habe ich dieses ganze Volk gezeugt?
Did I conceive all this people?

(Gb↕:Db = Db↕ : Db)

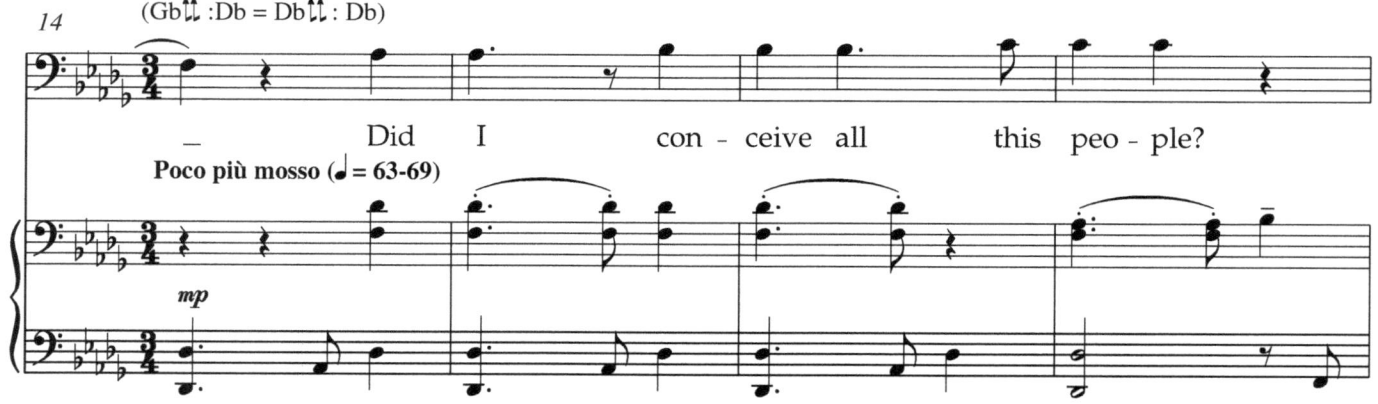

Did I con - ceive all this peo - ple?

Poco più mosso (♩ = 63-69)

mp

(28) Habe ich es denn geboren?
Did I bring them forth, all this people?

Did I bring them forth, all this peo - ple?

(29) Habe ich es auf meinem Schoß getragen?
Did I carry them on my bosom?

Did I car - ry them on my _____ bo - som?

(30) Habe ich es genährt?
Did I nurse them?

(31) Warum hast du deinen Diener schlecht behandelt?
Why hast thou dealt ill with thy servant?

(32) Sie weinen zu mir, dein Volk.
They weep unto me, your people.

(33) Woher sollte ich Fleisch für all dieses Volk haben?
Whence should I have flesh for all this people?

(34) Ich kann sie nicht auf meinen Schultern tragen,
I can not carry them on my shoulders,

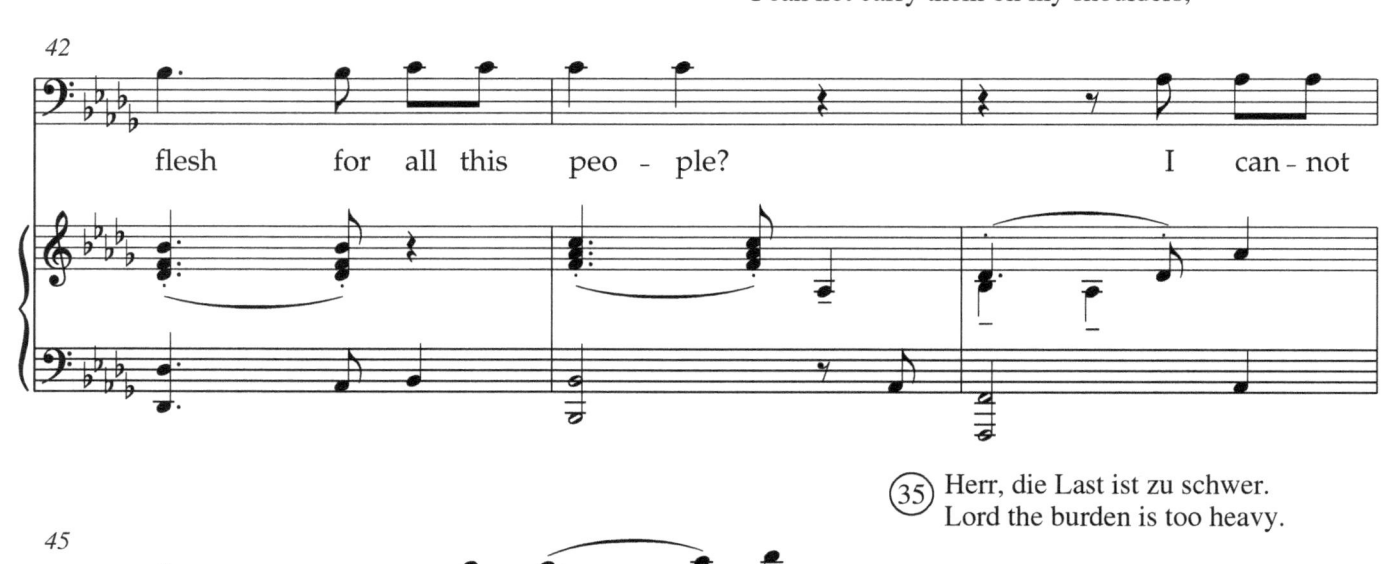

flesh for all this peo - ple? I can - not

(35) Herr, die Last ist zu schwer.
Lord the burden is too heavy.

car - ry them on my _____ shoul - ders, Lord, the

bur - den is too hea - vy.

(36) Wenn du so mit deinem Knecht umgehen willst,
If thou wilt thus deal with thy servant,

Tempo I

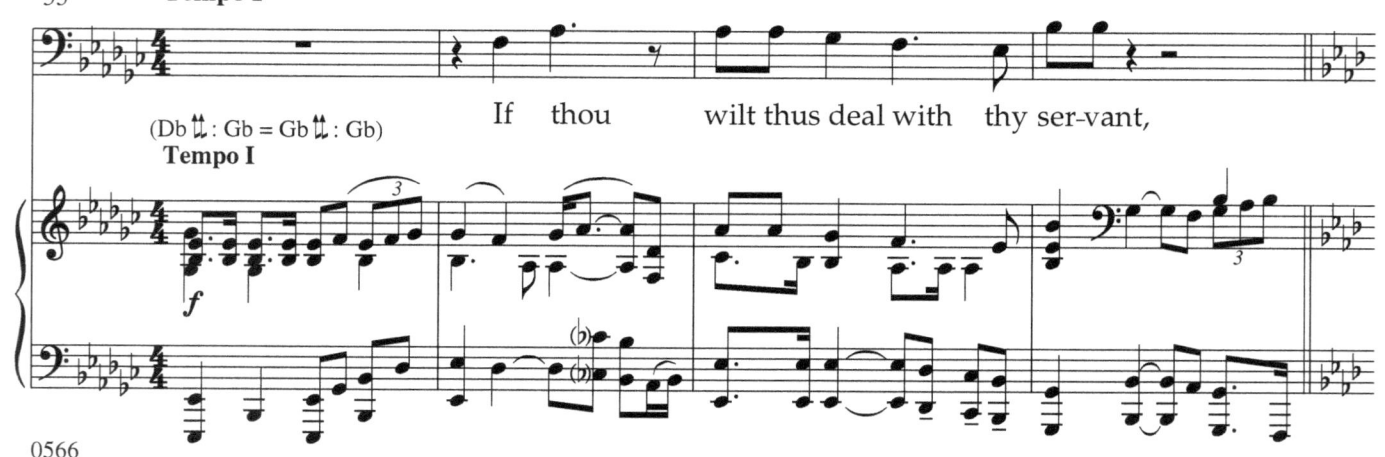

If thou wilt thus deal with thy ser-vant,

(Db ♮♮ : Gb = Gb ♮♮ : Gb)
Tempo I

(37) Wenn ich Gnade gefunden habe in deinen Augen
If I have found favor in thy sight

(38) denn solltest du mich töten
then thou shouldst kill me

(39) und beende dieses Elend.
and end this wretchedness.

(40) Warum hast du deinen Diener schlecht behandelt?
Why hast thou dealt ill with thy servant?

(41) Auf! Macht uns Götter, die vor uns hergehen!
Up! Make us gods who will go before us.

#24 Chorale Up! Make us gods

F♮ Allegro (♩. = ca 76)

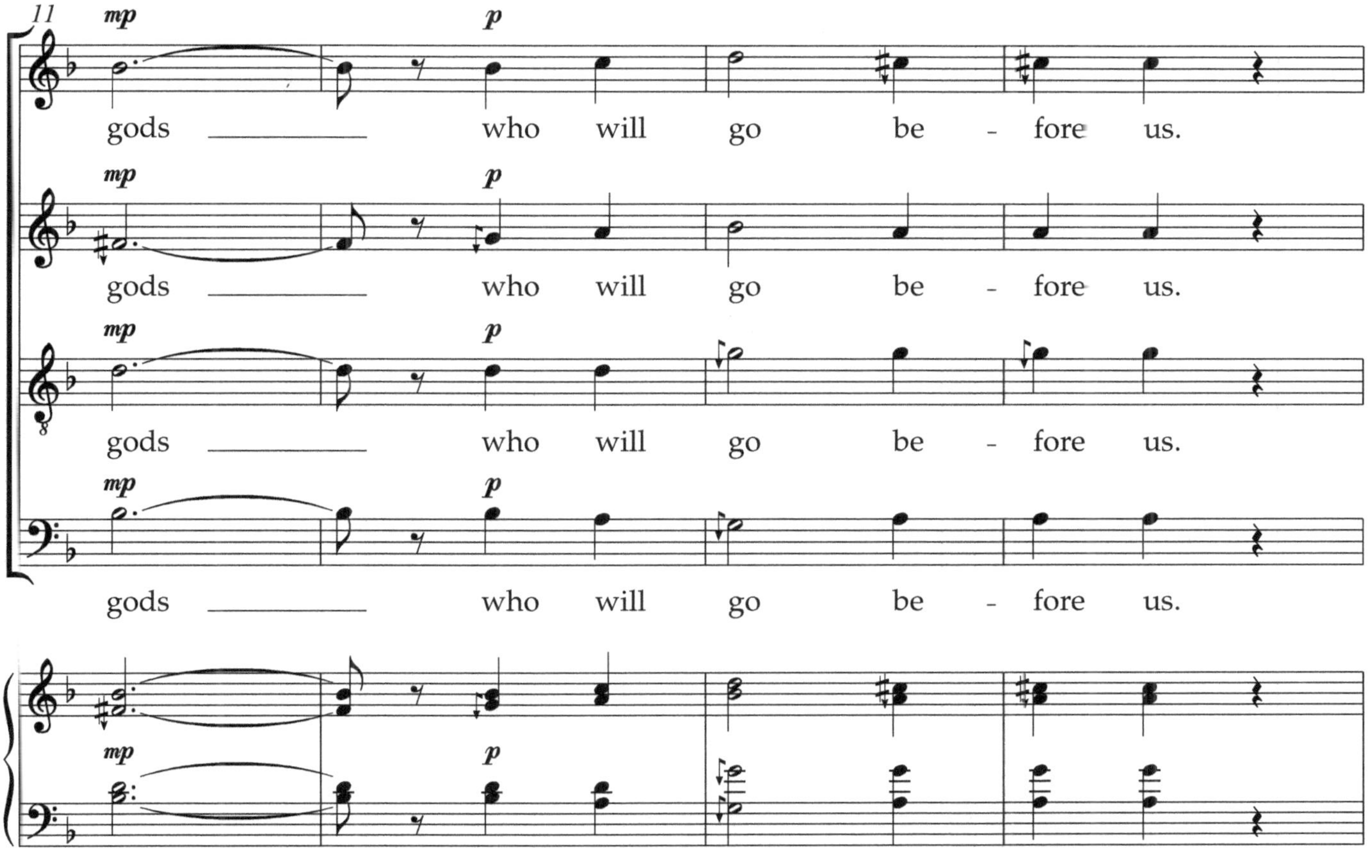

11

S: gods _____ who will go be - fore us.

A: gods _____ who will go be - fore us.

T: gods _____ who will go be - fore us.

B: gods _____ who will go be - fore us.

(42) Was Moses betrifft, wissen wir nicht.
As for Moses, we do not know.

15

S: As for Mo - ses, we do not know.

A: As for Mo - ses, we do not know.

T: As for Mo - ses, we do not know.

B: As for Mo - ses, we do not know.

#25 Chorus And the men who were the heads

(43) Und die Männer, die Häupter
And the men who were the heads

(44) des Volkes Israel waren
of the people of Israel

And the men who were the heads of the peo - ple of Is - ra-el

And the men who were the heads of the peo - ple of Is - ra-el

(45) kundschafteten das Land aus und sagten:
spied out the land, and said:

(46) dort sahen wir die Nephilim.
there we saw Nephilim.

spied out the land _ and said: there we saw Neph-i-lim.

spied out the land _ and said: there we saw Neph-i-lim.

(47) wir schienen uns selbst wie Heuschrecken.
we seemed like grasshoppers.

20

S: We seemed like grass-hop-pers, we seemed like

A: We seemed like grass-hop-pers, we seemed like

T:

B:

mf

27

S: grass - hop-pers.

A: grass - hop-pers.

T:

B:

f

#26 Chorus Would that we had died

48 Hätten wir doch gestorben.
Would that we had died.

49 Hätten wir doch dort im Land Ägypten gestorben.
Would that we had died there, in the land of Egypt.

50 Oder hier gestorben, hier in dieser Wüste.
Or that we had died here, here in this wilderness.

(51) Hätten wir dort gestorben, im Land Ägypten.
Would we had died there, the land of Egypt.

Allegro Furioso

(52) Oder hier gestorben, hier in dieser Wildnis.
Or would we'd died here, here in this wilderness.

(53) Warum führt uns der Herr in diese Wüste?
Why does the Lord bring us into this desert?

124

(54) Warum bringt uns alle hier,
Why bring us all here

(55) um durch das Schwert zu sterben?
to fall and die by the sword.

(56) Nehmt uns aus Milch un Honig, dem Land des Pharao,
Take us from milk and honey, land of the Pharaoh,

(57) tötet uns in der Wüste, unsere Kleinen werden zur Beute.
kill us in the wilderness our little ones will fall a prey.

0566

(58) Und dafür willst du dich erheben? Du willst ein Fürst sein?
And for this you would exalt yourself, you'd be a prince?

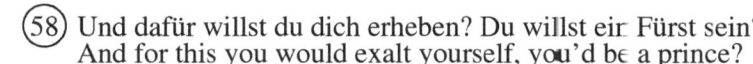

f

T: And for this __ you would ex - alt your-self, __ you'd be __

B: lit - tle ones will fall a prey, and for this __ you would ex - alt your-self, __ you'd be a

(59) Nehmt uns vom Pharao, dem Land aus Milch und Honig,
Take us from Pharaoh, the land of milk and honey,

S: Take us from Pha - raoh,

A: Take us from Pha - raoh,

T: _ a prince, _ a prince, _ a prince, _ a prince. Take us from Pha - raoh,

B: prince, prince, prince, prince, prince.

0566

126

S: the land of milk and ho - ney, in - to this

A: the land of milk and ho - ney, in - to this

T: the land of __ milk and ho - ney, in - to this

60 In diese Wüste, wir werden fallen und durch das Schwert sterben.
Into this desert, we'll fall and die by the sword.

S: des - ert, die, __ and die,

A: des - ert, we'll fall and die, __ and die,

T: des - ert, we'll fall and die, fall and die by the

B: we'll fall and die,

0566

(61) Nehmt uns aus Milch und Honig, dem Land des Pharao,
Take us from milk and honey, land of the Pharaoh,

(62) Und in der Wildnis zur Beute aller werden.
And in the wilderness all to fall a prey.

(63) Du, Mose, hast es zu weit getrieben.
You, Moses, have gone too far.

C566

far, have gone too far, have gone too far.

far, far,___ have gone too far.

far, have gone too far, too far.___

far, have gone too far.___

(64) Jeder in der Gemeinde ist heilig, jeder von ihnen,
Every one of the congregation is holy, every one of them,

(65) und der Herr ist unter ihnen,
and the Lord is among them,

Ev'-ry one of the con-gre-ga-tion is ho-ly, ev'-ry one of them, and the Lord is a-mong them,

Ev'-ry one of the con-gre-ga-tion is ho-ly, ev'-ry one of them, and the Lord is a-mong them,

Ev'-ry one of the con-gre-ga-tion is ho-ly, ev'-ry one of them, and the Lord is a-mong them,

Ev'-ry one of the con-gre-ga-tion is ho-ly, ev'-ry one of them, and the Lord is a-mong them,

66 jeder von ihnen, Mose.
every one of them, Moses.

67 Mose, du hast es zu weit getrieben.
Moses you have gone too far.

63

S: you have gone too, you have gone too far.

A: you have gone too, you have gone too far.

T: you have gone too, you have gone too far.

B: you have gone too, you have gone too far.

(Fl)

68 Warum hast du uns in diese Wüste gebracht?
Why did you bring us into this desert?

66

S: Why did you bring us

A: Why did you bring us

T: Why did you bring us

B: Why did you bring us

(Bsn.)

(Eb: Ab = Ab: Ab)

(69) Warum müssen wir hier sterben, hier in dieser Wildnis?
Why must we die here, here in this wilderness?

71

S: in – to this des – – ert? Why must we

A: in – to this des – – ert? Why must we

T: in – to this des – – ert? Why must we

B: in – to this des – – ert? Why must we

(70) Nehmt uns aus Milch und Honig, dem Land des Pharao,
Take us from milk and honey, land of the Pharaoh,

74

cresc. *f*

S: die here, here in this wil – der-ness? Take us!

A: die here, here in this wil – der-ness? Take us from milk and ho-ney,

T: die here, here in this wil – der-ness? Take us from milk and ho-ney,

B: die here, here in this wil – der-ness? Take us

0566

(71) tötet uns in die Wüste, unsere Kleinen werden zu Beute,
kill us in the wilderness, our little ones will fall a prey,

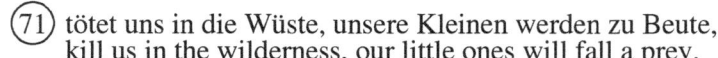

S — *(rest)* — Kill us! — *(rest)*

A — land of the Pha - raoh, kill us in the wil-der-ness, our lit - tle ones will fall a prey,

T — land of the Pha - raoh, __ kill us in the wil-der-ness, our lit - tle ones will fall a prey,

B — Kill us!

(Fl)

(72) und dafür willst du dich erheben, du willst ein Fürst sein.
and for this you would exalt yourself, you'd be a prince.

f

S — and for this __ you would ex - alt your-self, __ you'd be a prince.

A — and for this __ you would ex - alt your-self, __ you'd be ___ a prince, __ a prince, __ a prince, __ a prince.

T — and for this __ you would ex - alt your-self, __ you'd be a prince, prince, prince, prince,

B — *(rest)*

f *poco* f

f f

(73) Bring uns zurück nach Ägypten, Mose!
Take us back to Egypt, Moses!

(74) Lasst uns nach Ägypten zurückkehren!
Let us go back to Egypt!

(75) Du, Mose, hast es zu weit getrieben.
You Moses have gone too far.

0566

(76) Hätten wir doch gestorben.
Would that we had died.

that we had

that we had

that we had

we had

died, had died, had

died, had died, had

died, would that we had

died, had died, had

PART VI. Face to Face: I brought you on eagles' wings

(77) Und Mose stieg hinauf zu Gott
And Moses went up to God

#27 Recitative And Moses went up

F♮ **Moderato** (♩=84)

(78) und der Herr rief ihn aus dem Berge und sprach:
and the Lord called him out of the mountain, saying:

#28 Chorale Eagles, on eagles

A Andante ($\quarternote$ = 80-88)

(79) Adler, auf Adlern,
Eagles, on eagles,

(80) auf starken Adlerflügeln habe ich euch getragen.
on eagles' strong wings I brought you.

(81) Ihr sollt mein Volk aller Nationen sein, (82) von allen sollt ihr mein Volk sein.
You shall be my people of all the nations. you shall be my people of all.

S: ea-gles' strong wings. You shall, you shall be my peo-ple of all the na-tions, you shall, you

A: ea-gles' strong wings. You shall, you shall be my peo-ple of all the na-tions, you shall, you

T: ea-gles' strong wings. You shall, you shall be my peo-ple of all the na-tions, you shall, you

B: ea-gles' strong wings. You shall, you shall be my peo-ple of all the na-tions, you shall, you

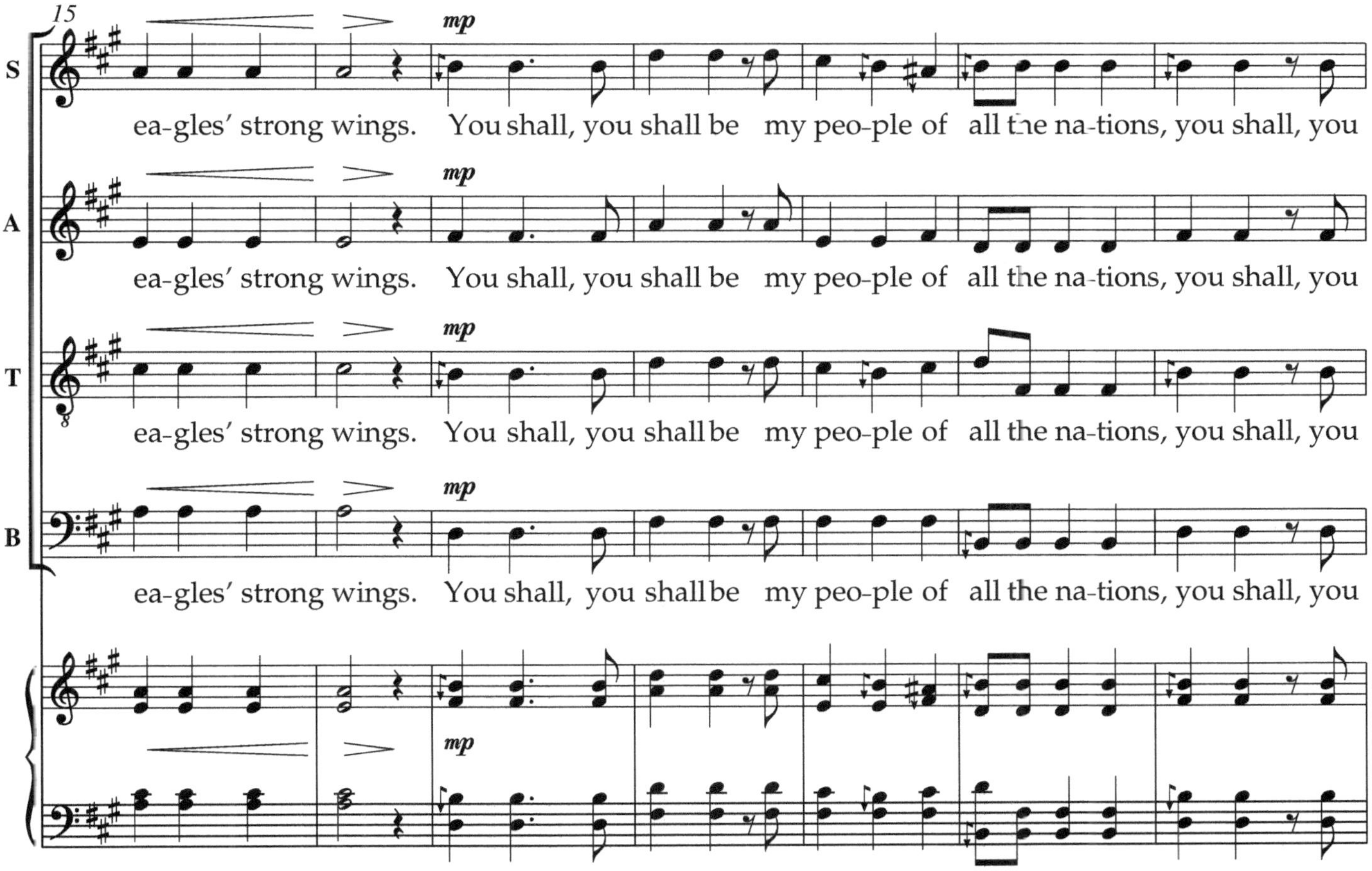

(83) Auf starken Adlerflügeln habe ich euch getragen.
On eagles' strong wings I brought you.

S: shall be my peo-ple of all. Oh, ea-gles, on ea-gles, on ea-gles' strong wings.

A: shall be my peo-ple of all.

T: shall be my peo-ple of all. Oh, ea-gles, on ea-gles' strong wings.

B: shall be my peo-ple of all.

(84) Ihr sollt mein Volk aller Nationen sein.
You shall be my people of all the nations.

#29 Chorus Give ear, o ye heavens

(85) Gebt Ohren, ihr Himmel, und ich werde sprechen, (86) Hört, o Gott, die Worte meines Mundes,
Give ear, O ye heavens, and I will speak; Hear, o God, the words of my mouth,

(87) Meine Lehre werde fallen wie der Regen, (88) Mein Geist werde tauen wie der Tau,
My doctrine shall drop as the rain, My spirit shall distill as the dew,

(89) Wie leichter Regen auf das zarte Kraut, (90) wie Schauer auf das Gras.
Like small rain on the tender herb, as showers on the grass.

Give ear, O ye hea-vens, I will speak;

Hear, O God, the words of my mouth.

Hear, O God, the words of my mouth. My doc-trine shall drop as the

Hear, O God, the words of my mouth. My doc-trine shall drop as the

My spi-rit shall dis-till as the dew.

rain.

rain.

91 Schreibt unserem Gott Größe zu,
Ascribe ye greatness unto our God,

poco rit.

Poco più mosso

A - scribe ye

A - scribe ye

(Tpt.)
(Fl.)

poco rit.

Poco più mosso ($\quarternote$ =96-104)

92 Der Fels, dessen Werk vollkommen ist;
Who is the rock, whose work is perfect;

great - ness un - to our God who is the rock whose work is

great - ness un - to our God who is the rock whose work is

0566

(93) Denn all seine Wege sind gerecht.
for all God's ways are judgment.

(94) Screibt unserem Gott Größe zu,
Ascribe ye greatness unto our God,

(95) Einem Gott der Wahrheit und ohne Unrect.
A God of truth and without iniquity.

(96) Schreibt unserem Gott Größe zu
Ascribe ye greatness unto our God

(97) Der fels, dessen Werk vollkommen ist;
Who is the rock, whose work is perfect;

146

(98) Denn all seine Wege sing gerecht.
for all God's ways are judgment.

0566

E: A God of truth, a

S: out in - i - qui - ty, a - scribe ye great - ness. A God of truth, a

A: out in - i - qui - ty, a - scribe ye great - ness. A God of truth, a

T: out in - i - qui - ty, a - scribe ye great - ness. A God of truth, a

B: out in - i - qui - ty, a - scribe ye great - ness. A God of truth, a

E: God of truth and with-out in - i - qui - ty,

S: God of truth and with-out in - i - qui - ty, a

A: God of truth and with-out __ in - i - qui - ty, a

T: God of truth and with-out in - i - qui - ty, a - scribe ye great-ness, a

B: God of truth and with out in - i - qui - ty, a - scribe ye great-ness, a

God of truth and with-

out in- - i- - qui- - ty, a-scribe ye

a-scribe ye

great - ness, a - scribe ye great - ness, un-to our

great - ness, a - scribe ye great - ness, a - scribe ye great - ness un-to our

great - ness, a - scribe ye great - ness, a - scribe ye great - ness un-to our

great - ness, a - scribe ye great - ness, a - scribe ye great - ness un-to our

great - ness, a - scribe ye great - ness, a - scribe ye great - ness un-to our

God.

God.

God.

God.

God.

#30 Paean For ask now
Moderato

The Ecstatic

Men's Chorus

Orchestra Reduction

B♭ Moderato (♩=84)

(99) Denn fragt nun, (100) Fragt nach den vergangenen Tagen, (101) Seitdem Gott den Menschen erschaffen hat;
For ask now, Ask of the days that are past since the days that God created man;

E

For _ ask _ now, _ ask _ of the days _ that are past, since the days that God cre-at-ed

BASSES

B

Ask, ask,

(102) Fragt von einem Ende des Himmels bis zum anderen, (103) ob je etwas so Großes geschehen ist,
Ask from one side of the heavens to the other   whether there has been any such thing

man. Ask from one side of the hea-vens to the oth-er   whe-ther there has been an-y such

ask,   ask.

(104) Wie dieses große Geschehen. (105) Es erhob sich kein Prophet mehr wie Mose,
as is this great thing.   There arose not a prophet like unto Moses

thing as is this great thing.   There a - rose not a

(106) Den der Herr von Angesicht zu Angesicht kannte.
whom the Lord knew face to face.

(107) Mein Diener Mose,
My servant Moses,

(108) Den ich von Angesicht zu Angesicht kannte,
whom I knew face to face,

(109) Ihm ist mein ganzes Haus anvertraut.
He is entrusted with all my house.

110 Es erhob sich kein Prophet mehr wie Mose,
There arose not a prophet like unto Moses

111 den der Herr von Angesicht zu Angesicht kannte.
whom the Lord knew face to face.

PART VII. Miriam Sang: Sing to the Lord gloriously

#31 **Celebration** Sing to the Lord

Allegro
Moses
Allegro
Soprano
Alto
Tenor
Bass
G Allegro (♩.=84)

112 Eia, eia, eia!
Eia, eia, eia!
Mos
S
E - ia, e-ia, e - ia-a - a - a-a, e - ia, e-
A
E - ia, e-ia, e - ia-a - a - a-a, e - ia, e-
T
B
(Br.,Ww.)

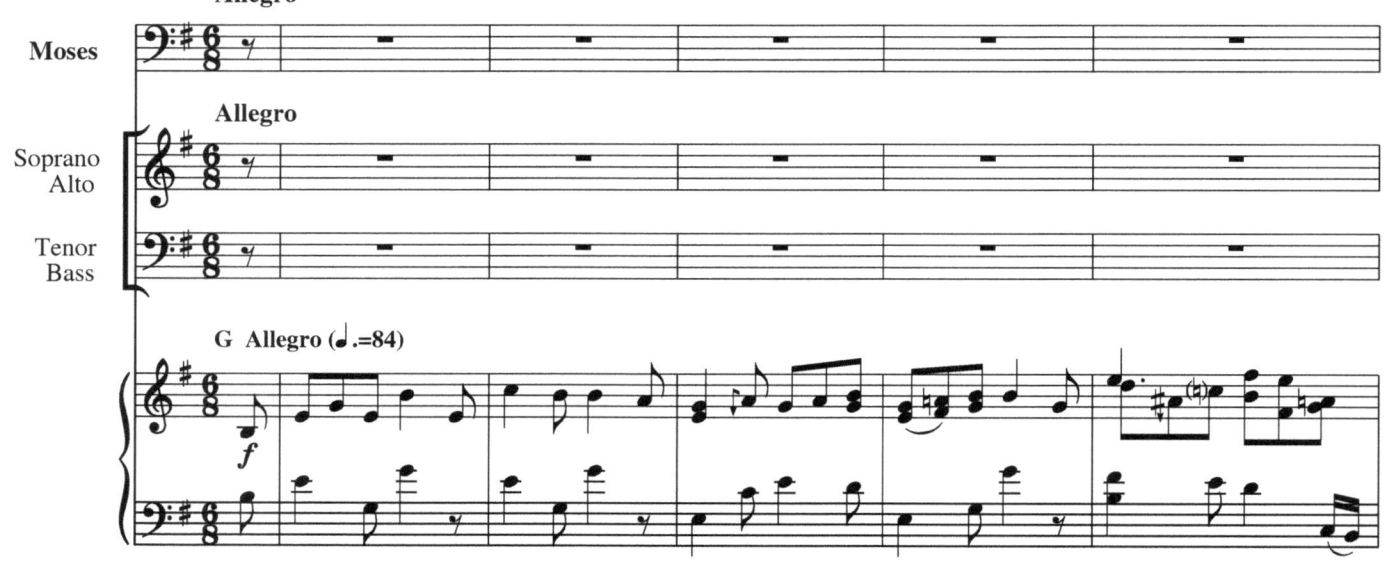

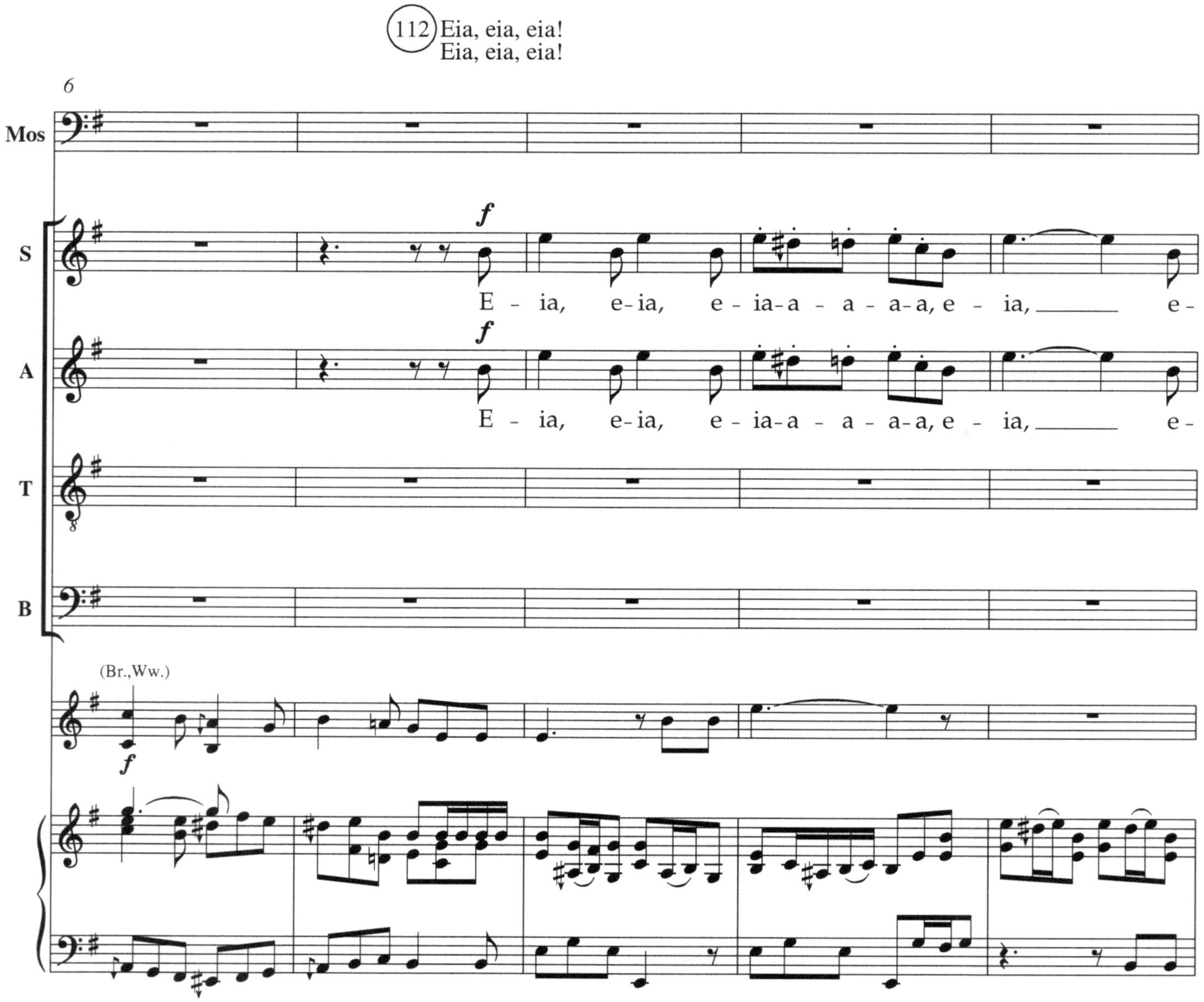

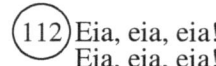

113 Singt dem Herrn!
Sing to the Lord!

(114) Singt dem Herrn, überwinden,
Sing to the Lord, overcoming,

(115) die Glorie, glorreich, glorreich,
Glory, glorious, gloriously,

(116) Pferd und Reiter kippen um,
Horse and rider overturning,

(117) rüber ins Meer.
over into the sea.

Glory, glo-ri-ous, glo-ri-ous-ly.

Mos

S: glo-ry, glo-ri-ous, glo-ri-ous-ly. Horse and ri - der o - ver turn - ing o - ver in-to the

A: glo-ry, glo-ri-ous, glo-ri-ous-ly. Horse and ri - der o - ver turn - ing o - ver in-to the

T: Glo-ry, glo-ri-ous-ly. Horse and ri - der o - ver turn - ing o - ver in-to the

B: Glo-ry, glo-ri-ous-ly. Glo-ry, glo-ri-ous, glo-ri-ous-ly.

(118) Singt dem Herrn, überwinden,
Sing to the Lord, overcoming,

(119) die Glorie, glorreich, glorreich,
Glory, glorious, gloriously,

(120) Pferd und Reiter kippen um
Horse and rider overturning

53

Mos

S: sea. Sing to the Lord, o-ver-com-ing, glo-ry, glo-ri-ous, glo-ri-ous-ly. Horse and ri - der

A: sea. Sing to the Lord, o-ver-com-ing, glo-ry, glo-ri-ous, glo-ri-ous-ly. Horse and ri - der

T: sea.

B:

121 rüber ins Meer.
over into the sea.

Mos

S
o-ver turn-ing, o-ver in-to the sea. ___ E- ia, _____ a a a a, e - ia, e- ia, _____

A
o-ver turn-ing, o-ver in-to the sea. ___

T

B

ia, a, a, a, _____ sing, sing.

A, a, a, _____ sing, ___ sing.

Sing to the Lord.

Sing to the Lord. Sing to the Lord,

71

Mos

S

A

T

o- ver-com-ing glo-ry, glo-ri-ous, glo-ri-ous-ly. Horse and ri- der o- ver turn-ing o- ver in-to the

B

77

Mos

E- ia! _____

S

Sing to the Lord,   sing to the Lord.   O - ver -

A

Sing to the Lord.   sing to the Lord.   O - ver -

T

sea.

Sing to the Lord.   O - ver -

B

Sing to the Lord.   O - ver -

Mos: E - ia!

S: turn - ing o - ver in-to the sea. Sing, sing! Sing,

A: turn - ing o - ver in-to the sea. Sing, sing!

T: turn - ing o - ver in-to the sea. Sing, sing! Sing,

B: turn - ing o - ver in-to the sea.

S: sing! Sing sing.

A: Sing, sing! Sing sing.

T: sing!

Sing, sing, sing sing to the Lord.

Sing, sing, sing, sing, sing, sing to the Lord.

Sing to the Lord, o - ver-com-ing, glo - ry, glo-ri- ous, glo-ri- ous-ly. Horse and ri - der

Sing to the Lord, o - ver-com-ing, glo - ry, glo-ri- ous, glo-ri- ous-ly. Horse and ri - der

o-ver-turn-ing, o-ver in-to the sea. ___ Ei - ia, ___ a, a, a, a, ei-

o-ver-turn-ing, o-ver in-to the sea. ___ Ei - ia, ___ ei-

ia! ___

ia! ___

#32 Scene Behold I will strike the water

122 Siehe, ich will die Wasser im Nil treffen.
Behold I will strike the waters which are in the Nile.

Be-hold: I will strike the wa - ters which are in the

(123) Und alle Wasser verwandelten sich in Blut,
And all the waters turned into blood,

(124) alle Wasser, die im Nil waren.
all the waters which were in the Nile.

(125) Singt dem Herrn.
Sing to the Lord.

166

(126) Und die Frösche kamen heraus und bedeckten das Land.
And the frogs came up and covered the land.

(127) Und die Frösche kamen heraus
And the frogs came up

(128) und die Frösche kamen über das Land.
and the frogs came over the land.

0566

(129) Streck deinen Stab aus und schlag den Staub von der Erde
Stretch out your rod and strike dust from the earth

59

Mos

S

f

Stretch out your rod and strike dust from the earth that it

A

Stretch out your rod and strike dust from the earth that it

T

Stretch out your rod and strike dust from the earth that it

B

Stretch out your rod and strike dust from the earth that it

(Bb♮ : C = C♮ : C)

f

(130) damit es zu Läusen wird.
that it may become lice.

63

S

may be-come lice.

A

may be-come lice.

T

may be-come lice.

B

may be-come lice.

(C♮ : B = B: B)

f

(131) Dann kam ein schlimmer Fliegenschwarm.
Then there came a grievous swarm of flies.

S: Then there came a griev-ous swarm of flies.

A: Then there came a griev-ous swarm of flies, swarm of flies, swarm of flies.

T: Then there came a griev-ous swarm of flies, swarm of flies, swarm of flies.

B: Then there came a griev-ous swarm of flies, swarm of flies, swarm of flies.

(132) Singt dem Herrn.
Sing to the Lord.

(133) Siehe, da sandte die Hand des Herrn eine sehr schwere Plage
Behold the hand of the Lord then sent a very severe plague

(134) auf alle Rinder, die auf den Feldern waren.
on all the cattle which were in the fields.

(135) das ganze Vieh ist gestorben.
all the cattle died.

(136) Nimm die Hände voll Staub und es wird zu Furunkeln.
Take handsful of dust and it shall become boils.

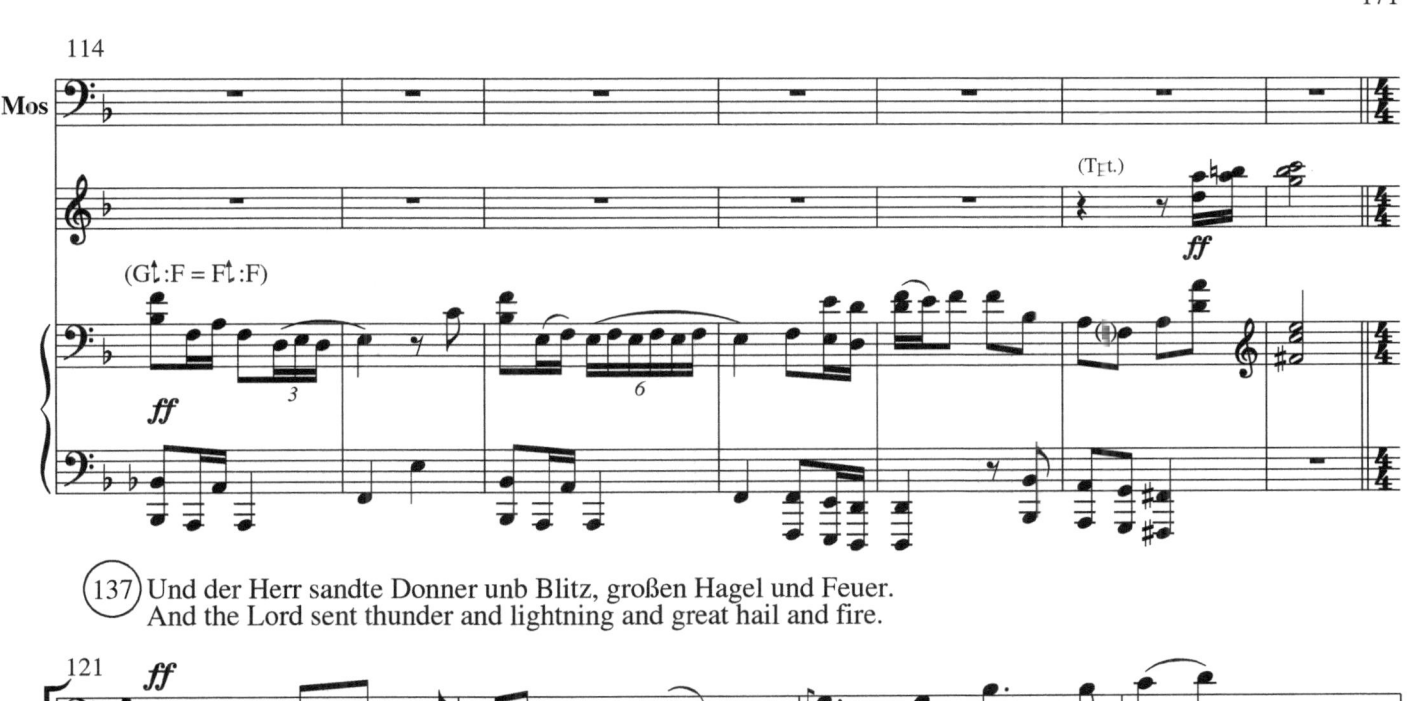

(137) Und der Herr sandte Donner unb Blitz, großen Hagel und Feuer.
And the Lord sent thunder and lightning and great hail and fire.

And the Lord sent thun - der and light-ning and great hail and fire, ___

And the Lord sent thun - der and light-ning and great hail and fire, ___ the Lord sent

Thun - der, fire, the Lord sent ___ light-ning and great hail and fire, _____ sent

Mos

S: And the Lord sent thun - der and light - ning and great hail and

A: And the Lord sent thun-

S: fire, _____ great hail and

A: - der and light - ning, and great hail and fire, _____ great hail and

S: fire, the Lord sent thun-der, light-ning and great hail and fire. __

A: fire, the Lord sent thun-der, light-ning and __ great hail and fire, __ fire, _

T: And the Lord sent thun - der and light-ning and great hail and fire. __

A: thun-der.

B: And the Lord sent thun - der and light - ning and great hail, great hail __ and

155

T: And the Lord sent thun - der and light - ning,

B: fire, ___ fire. ___

158

T: great hail and fire, great hail, and great hail and

B: And the Lord sent thun - der and light - ning, and great hail and

S: fire, — fire.

A: Fire, great hail and fire, great hail and fire, great hail and fire.

T: fire. Fire, fire,

B: fire. Fire, fire,

Mos: The Lord sent

S: The Lord sent

A: The Lord sent

T: fire. Fire, fire, fire. The Lord sent

B: fire. Fire, — fire, fire. The Lord sent

(F ♮: Bb = Bb ♮: Bb)

Mos: thun-der, light-ning, hail, great hail.

S: thun-der, light-ning, hail, great hail.

A: thun-der, light-ning, hail, great hail.

T: thun-der, light-ning, hail, great hail.

B: thun-der, light-ning, hail, great hail.

#33 Scene How long refuse us?

138 Wie lange verweigern wir uns?
How long refuse us?

139 Wie lange weigern sie sich, uns gehen zu lassen?
How long refuse to let us go?

How long re-fuse us?   How long re-fuse to let us go?

How long re-fuse us?   How long re-fuse to let us go?

(140) So spricht der Herr: Wie lange?
Thus sayth the Lord, how long?

(141) Wie lange weigern sich meine Leute,
How long refuse my people,

(142) Wie lange weigern, sie gehen zu lassen?
How long refuse to let them go?

(143) So spricht der Herr: Wie lange?
Thus sayth the Lord, how long?

(144) Wie lange weigern sich unsere Leute?
How long refuse our people?

(145) Wie lange weigern sie sich, uns gehen zu lassen?
How long refuse to let us go?

(146) So spricht der Herr: Wie lange?
Thus say'th the Lord, how long?

(147) Wie lange verweigern wir uns?
How long refuse us?

(148) Wie lange weigern sie sich, uns gehen zu lassen?
How long refuse to let us go?

0566

(149) Ich werde Heuschrecken ins Land bringen,
I will bring locusts into the country,

(150) Und sie werden alles überdecken,
And they will cover over,

184

(151) Für sie wird niemand das Land sehen.
for them no one will see the land.

(152) Heuschrecken! Heuschrecken!
Locusts! Locusts!

(153) Sie werden es überdecken,
They will cover over,

(154) für sie wird niemand das Land sehen.
for them no one will see the land.

0566

land.

land.

How long re-fuse us, how long re-fuse to let us go?

How long re-fuse us, how long re-fuse to let us go?

How long re-fuse us, how long re-fuse to let us go?

155 Und sie werden fressen, was übrig ist
And they will eat all that is left

156 Nach dem Hagel.
after the hail.

#34 **March** Darkness

157 Dunkelheit, Dunkelheit.
Darkness, darkness.

158 Schwere Dunkelheit, Dunkelheit.
Heavy darkness, darkness.

159 Schwere Dunkelheit
Heavy dark,

Dark- ness,

Hea-vy dark - ness, dark-ness.

Hea - vy

Hea-vy dark - ness, dark-ness.

Hea - vy

dark-ness.

Hea - vy dark - ness, dark-ness.

0566

160 Dunkelheit, die man spüren kann.
Dark that can be felt.

161 Dunkelheit: Man kann sie spüren.
Darkness: it can be felt.

(162) Da sagte der Pharao: Geh weg, geh!
Then Pharaoh said, Get away, go,

28

E

Then Pha-raoh said, said, "Get a-way, go". _ "Get a-way,

Mcs

_ dark-ness.

(163) du wirst mein Gesicht nie wieder sehen.
never see my face again.

34

E

go, _ ne-ver see my face a-gain: go, go." Pha-raoh said,

Mos

T

said ne-ver see my face. _ Pha-raoh

B

Pha-raoh

164 Wie du wünscht.
As you say.

(165) Ich werde dein Gesicht nicht mehr sehen.
I will not see your face again.

169 In Ägypten gab es einen großen Aufschrei.
There was a great cry in Egypt.

#36 Scene Then did Pharaoh's daughter

F↕ Adagietto (♩ = 63-66)
Soprano
Alto
Tenor
Bass
Orchestra
Reduction
f
rit.
p
mp
a tempo
p
mp
170 Dann handelte die Tochter des Pharaos
Then did Pharaoh's daughter
S
mf pp
Then
p
mf
mp
sf
p
171 erziehe ihn zu ihrem Sohn.
bring him up to be her son.
172 Sie nannte ihn Moses,
she called him Moses,
S
mp dolce
f
did Pha-raoh's daugh-ter bring him up to be her son, she called him Mo - ses,
dolce
mp
f

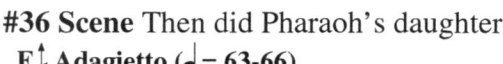

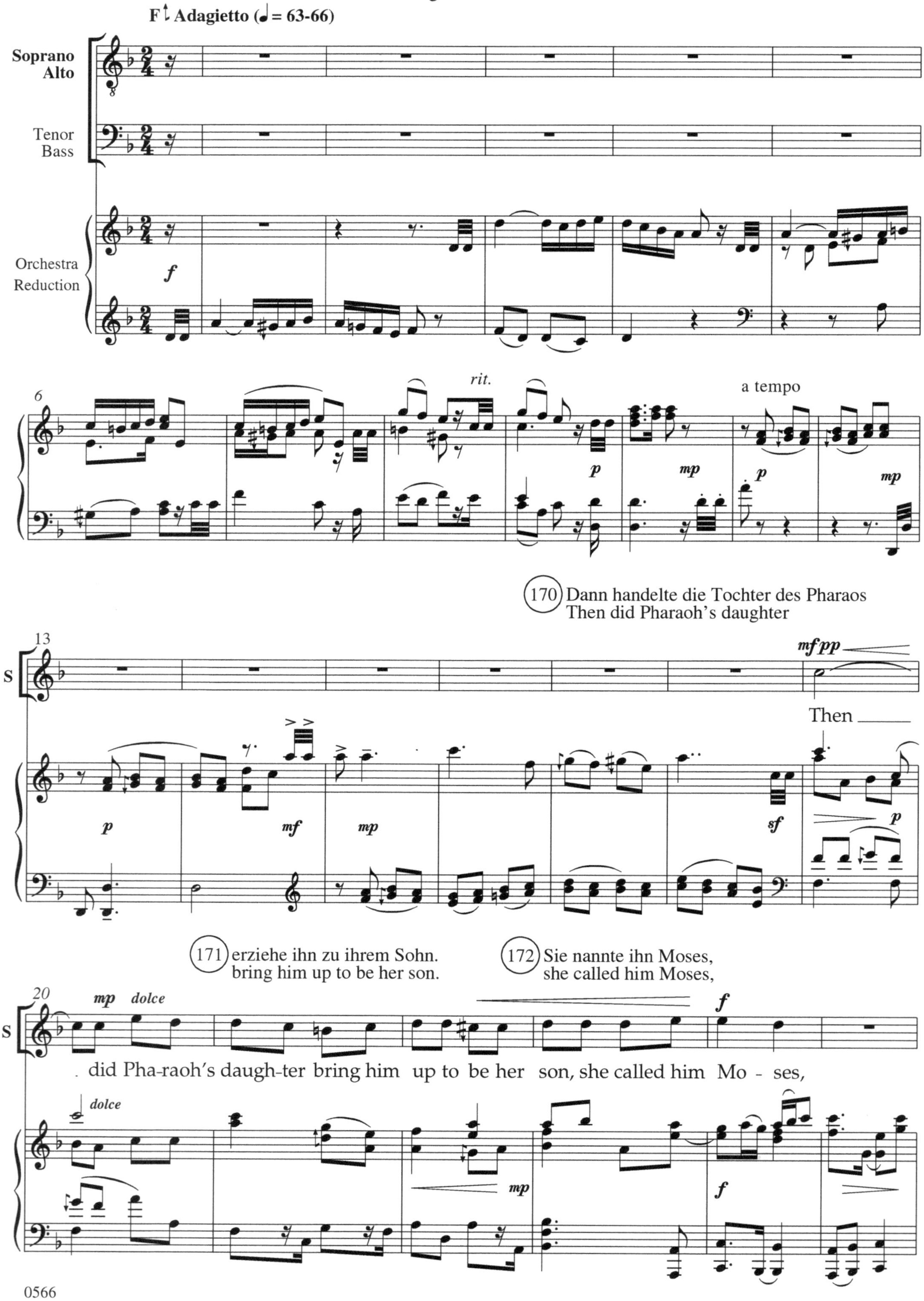

(173) Sie nannte ihn bei seinem Namen Moses.
She called his name Moses.

(174) Sie sagte: Ich habe ihn aus dem Wasser gezogen.
She said, I drew him from the waters.

S: Mo - ses, she called his name Mo - ses. She said I drew him from the wa - ters,

A: Mo - ses, she called his name Mo - ses. She said I drew him from the wa - ters,

T: I drew him from the wa - ters,

S: from the wa - ters, from the wa - ters, said, I drew him from the wa - ters, from the wa - ters,

A: from the wa - ters, from the wa - ters, said, I drew him from the wa - ters, from the wa - ters,

T: from the wa - ters, from the wa - ters, said, from the wa - ters, said,

B: I drew him from the wa - ters, from the wa - ters,

S *38* *f*
from the wa-ters, said, I drew him from the wa-ters, from the wa-ters,

A
from the wa-ters, said, I drew him from the wa-ters, from the wa-ters,

T
from the wa-ters, said, I drew him from the wa-ters, from the wa-ters,

B
from the wa-ters, said, I drew him from the wa-ters, from the wa-ters,

(175) Geh hinauf, und sieh das gute Land.
Go up, and see the good land.

S *42* *ff*
from the wa-ters, Mo - - ses!

A *ff*
from the wa-ters, Mo - - ses! Go up, — and see the

T *ff*
from the wa-ters, Mo - - ses!

B *ff*
from the wa-ters, Mo - - ses!

S: Go up, and see the good land, the

A: good land. Go up and see the good land, the good land,

176) Ich nannte ihn Mose, ich zog ihn aus dem Wasser.
I called him Moses, I drew him from the waters.

S: good land, the good land. I called him Mo - ses, I drew him from the wa-ters.

A: good land, the good land. I called him Mo - ses, I drew him from the wa-ters.

177) She said, I drew him from the waters.
Sie sagte: ich habe ihn aus dem Wasser gezogen.

S: from the wa-ters, from the wa-ters, said I drew him from the wa-ters, from the wa-ters,

A: from the wa-ters, from the wa-ters, said I drew him from the wa-ters, from the wa-ters,

T: from the wa-ters, from the wa-ters, said I drew him from the wa-ters, from the wa-ters,

B: from the wa-ters, from the wa-ters, said I drew him from the wa-ters, from the wa-ters,

S: from the wa-ters, said I drew him from the wa-ters, from the wa-ters, from the wa-ters,

A: from the wa-ters, said I drew him from the wa-ters, from the wa-ters, from the wa-ters,

T: from the wa-ters, said I drew him from the wa-ters, from the wa-ters, from the wa-ters,

B: from the wa-ters, said I drew him from the wa-ters, from the wa-ters, from the wa-ters,

S: Mo - ses, Mo-ses! Mo - ses, Mo-ses!

A: Mo - ses, Mo-ses! Mo - ses, Mo-ses!

T: Mo-ses! Mo - ses, Mo - ses! Mo - ses, Mo - ses!

B: Mo-ses! Mo - ses, Mo - ses!

(178) Geh nach oben. Du sollst zu deinem Volk versammelt werden.
Go up. You shall be gathered to your people.

Allegro

S: Go up, _____ go up, go up, go up. You shall be gath-er'd to your

A: Go up, _____ go up, go up, go _ up. You shall be gath-er'd to your

T: Go up, go up, go up. You shall be gath-er'd to your

B: Go up, go up, go up. You shall be gath-er'd to your

(G: ♮Eb = Eb♮: Eb) Allegro (♩ = 120)

S: peo-ple, Mo-ses. Mo-ses, you shall be gath-er'd, you shall be gath-er'd to your

A: peo-ple, Mo-ses. Mo-ses, you shall be gath-er'd, you shall be gath-er'd to your

T: peo-ple, Mo-ses, Mo-ses you shall be gath-er'd, shall be gath-er'd to your

B: peo-ple, Mo-ses, Mo-ses you shall be gath-er'd, shall be gath-er'd to your

S: peo - ple, Mo - ses! Go up, Mo - ses.

A: peo - ple, Mo - ses! Go up, Mo - ses.

T: peo - ple, Mo - ses!

B: peo - ple, Mo - ses!

S: Go up, Mo-ses, go up, Mo-ses, go up, Mo - ses, you shall be gath-er'd to your

A: Go up, Mo-ses, go up, Mo-ses, go up, Mo - ses, you shall be gath-er'd to your

T: Mo - ses, go up. You shall be gath-er'd to your

B: Mo - ses, you shall be gath-er'd to your

S: peo - ple! Go up, you shall be gath-ered to your

A: peo - ple! Go up, you shall be gath-ered to your

T: peo - ple!

B: peo - ple!

Più mosso

(Eb♮ : D = D: D)

Più mosso (♩ =ca 132)

S: peo - ple, __ peo - ple, go up,

A: peo - ple, your peo - ple, go up, you shall be gath-ered to your

S: You shall be gath-ered to your peo - ple.

A: peo - ple. You shall be gath-er'd to your

T: Mo - ses! You shall be gath-ered to your peo - ple.

B: Mo - ses! You shall be gath-ered to your peo - ple.

poco a poco accel.

S: You shall be gath-er'd to your peo - ple!

A: peo - ple, gath-er'd to your peo - ple!

T: You shall be gath-er'd to your peo - ple, Mo - ses, you shall,

B: peo - ple, gath-er'd to your peo - ple! you shall, ____

poco a poco accel.

T: you shall be gath - er'd.

B: you ___ shall be gath - er'd.

(Tbn) *ff*

ff

Tenor: You, _____ you, Mo-ses, ycu.

Bass: You, _____ you, Mo-ses, ycu.

Soprano: Go up, go up, Mo - ses, you Mo - ses.

Alto: Go up, go up, Mo - ses, you Mo - ses.

Tenor: You, you, you, Mo - ses, you.

Bass: You, you, you, Mo - ses, you.

125

S Gath-er'd to your peo - ple, gath-er'd to your peo - ple, gath - er'd, gath-er'd to your

A Gath-er'd to your peo - ple, gath-er'd to your peo - ple, gath - er'd, gath-er'd to your

T Mo-ses

B Mo-ses

129 Allegro assai

S peo-ple.

A peo-ple.

T Go up, Mo-ses, go, go up, Mo-ses, go.

B Go up, Mo-ses, go, go up, Mo-ses, go.

Allegro assai ($\quad$ =ca 144-148)

You shall be gath - er'd, gath - er'd, gath-er'd to your

You shall be gath - er'd, gath - er'd, gath-er'd to your

You, Mo - ses, shall be gath - er'd, you shall be

You, Mo - ses, shall be gath - er'd, you shall be

peo - ple. You, you shall be

peo - ple. You, Mo - ses, shall be gath - er'd, you shall be

go. Mo-ses! Mo - ses!

go. Mo-ses! Mo - ses!

Mo-ses! Mo - ses!

Mo-ses! Mo - ses!

You shall be gath - er'd to your

You shall be gath - er'd to your

You shall be gath - er'd to your

You shall be gath - er'd to your

peo - ple, Mo - ses, gath - er'd to your peo - ple.

Mo - - - - - ses!